COLLEGE FAITH

150 Adventist Leaders
Share Faith Stories
from their College Days

Edited by
RONALD ALAN KNOTT

Pacific Press Publishing Association
Boise, Idaho
Oshawa, Ontario, Canada

Edited by Ronald Alan Knott
Designed by Dale Chapman
Cover art by Dale Chapman
Typeset in Galliard 11.5/14

Wide distribution of this book to Seventh-day Adventist college students
has been made possible, in part, by a grant from the Office of Education of
the North American Division of Seventh-day Adventists.

Unless otherwise indicated, Scripture references in this book are from the
King James Version. Other versions used:

The Clear Word
The Living Bible (TLB)
The Message
New American Standard Bible (NASB)
New English Version (NEV)
New International Version (NIV)
New King James Version (NKJV)
New Revised Standard Version (NRSV)
J. B. Phillips: *The New Testament in Modern English*
Revised Standard Version (RSV)
Today's English Version (TEV)
The Youth Bible

ISBN 0-8163-1322-9

95 96 97 98 99 • 5 4 3 2 1

CONTENTS

FOREWORD

You hold in your hands one of the most unusual books ever released by a Seventh-day Adventist publishing house. I have never seen anything quite like it and you probably haven't either. It is a truly amazing and moving collection of personal testimonies about real life.

As the title indicates, this book is all about college. These faith stories are written by people who reflect on spiritual lessons they learned during their higher education. The writers are people who are influential in determining what the Adventist Church is today—editors of our magazines, college and university presidents, hospital administrators, pastors, conference, union and General Conference leaders.

You will quickly discover, however, that you are not reading sermonettes from distant, unknown church officials. You are reading heartfelt testimonies of faith drawn from the young-adult experience of leaders today who were once college kids or grad students. You will read about the typical troubles and triumphs that are part of higher education: academic failure, financial crises, broken and mended social relationships, bad administrative decisions, model Christian teachers, rewards for simple faith, miraculous answers to prayer and shining moments of grace.

I know most of the writers personally, and have learned much from their stories here. I learn from Rosa Banks who credits the Holy Spirit with preventing her from participating in a tempting college prank that might well have gotten her thrown out of Oakwood College and undoubtedly changed her career. Rosa is one of my immediate colleagues as associate secretary of the North American Division.

I learn from G. Ralph Thompson, secretary of the General Conference, who as a young man at Caribbean Union College learned some painful lessons after getting caught up in a student strike. I learn from Bryan Breckenridge, who as a college freshman, got knocked to the ground while trying to separate two fighting businessmen, and learned a lesson about preferring others before oneself. Bryan is now president of two major Adventist hospitals.

I learn from Lyn Behrens, now president of Loma Linda University. As a young medical student, she agonized over a vital exam, and found a miracle of peace in a promise from the Scriptures contained in a "promise box" given her years before by an elementary school teacher. She aced the test.

I know of no other publication that puts a more human face on church leadership than this remarkable book.

Adventists in North America have historically placed a high priority on higher education, whether in our schools or elsewhere. Some who are leaders in our church today, and whose stories appear in this book, did not have the opportunity to attend Adventist colleges. God led them where they were. But in a special sense we know that so much of what the church is today has been determined in the classrooms, cafeterias, dorm rooms, chapels, work places and playing fields of Seventh-day Adventist colleges and universities. God works there. This book proves it.

I am pleased that the North American Division has been able to have a part in the wide distribution of *College Faith*. The Office of Education has subsidized the cost of the book for purchase by the colleges. At this writing, I am told that virtually every student and employee at Adventist colleges and universities in North America will receive a copy of *College Faith*. No Adventist book in recent history has received that circulation. I commend all parties, including Pacific Press as publisher, the Review and Herald as printer, and the colleges as buyers, for making it happen.

In the days ahead, thousands, young and old, will read this important book. My fervent prayer is that God will continue to work powerfully in the hearts of Adventist young people now as He has in the past, in Adventist schools and elsewhere. And as He does I know there will always be a wealth of material for inspiring future editions of *College Faith*.

Alfred C. McClure, President
The Seventh-day Adventist Church In North America
Silver Spring, Maryland

PREFACE

As with so many good things in my life these days, this book was my wife's idea.

Esther is associate pastor of Sligo Seventh-day Adventist Church in Takoma Park, Maryland. She has a special burden for the relationship between Sligo Church and the students and staff of Columbia Union College. Each year recently, she has arranged for the church to give the college students some small, meaningful gift at fall registration. In 1993, she raised $3000 from area churches so each student could receive a copy of Mark Finley's excellent little book *Studying Together*. In 1994, she asked Adventist pastors in the metropolitan Washington area to write short stories about spiritual lessons they learned during college. She collected about two dozen of those stories to put in a small booklet for the college students. When she asked about a title, I suggested "College Faith."

From that, it was a short, quick step to expanding her great idea into a much larger enterprise, and you hold in your hand the result.

The idea of *College Faith* hit home with me immediately. So much happens during college. Incredible growth takes place during those 48 months or so—growth that profoundly shapes the direction of life. The relationships, the crises, the shining moments of revelation we experience in college form patterns of thought that govern our way for years to come. With hardly any effort, my own "college faith" story played out easily in my mind. It's a simple story that I call "Sixteen Months of Fury and Faith." It goes like this.

In January, halfway through my junior year, the faculty director of the annual college play promised me the role of the "Stage Manager" in Thornton Wilder's play, *Our Town*, to be staged in April. I considered it the lead role, wanted it badly, and felt I got what I deserved. Then the director held general auditions, and, incredibly, gave the "Stage Manager" role to someone else. I was furious. Apologizing profusely for doing what he had to do, the director offered me the part of "George Gibbs," which I resented as typecasting, and hardly worthy of my great acting abilities. The fact that the director was my next-door neighbor, a close family friend, my department chairman and a fantastic teacher didn't stop me from hoping he'd feel as bad as possible about reneging on his promise. After a rather childish demonstration of wounded pride, I grudgingly accepted the "lesser" role.

In April came the yearbook crisis. I had my heart set on editing the *Minuteman* during my senior year. Having had, arguably, more staff experience on the book than any student on campus, I felt I deserved the honor. The faculty publications committee recommended only one name—mine—for the position. The Student Association constitution required the incoming SA president to select a name from among those recommended by the faculty publications committee. So I had it in the bag. But I had also very publicly supported the losing presidential candidate in the SA elections that spring. So I shouldn't have been surprised when the new president ignored the committee process and the constitution, and appointed someone else as editor. I, of course, was furious.

The following November, the education department required all senior secondary certification candidates to apply for student teaching positions in local schools. I filed my application early, determined to do my practicum at South Lancaster Academy. I had attended there myself; it was five minutes from my house; and I was terrified of being sent anywhere else, particularly to a public school. Incredibly, the faculty ignored my early application and, in February, sent me off to Tahanto Regional Public High School. Again, I was furious.

In a short and decisive period of my life, I had been dealt three bitter disappointments.

But God didn't leave it at that.

With a certain measure of spite, I threw myself into the role of "George Gibbs" in *Our Town*, and had a fabulous time. Of the eight college play productions I've been in, it was certainly my favorite role. And when the college paper printed its glowing review of the play, it even referred (incorrectly) to my character as the lead role.

In the fall, my senior classmates elected me president of the class, something they couldn't have done if I had been yearbook editor. I soon discovered that I had far more fun, a lot less stress, and learned many new things about leadership as an active class officer than I ever would have as editor of the yearbook.

As for the student teaching, I had a delightful time working with the public high school students during that last semester of college. The experience greatly broadened my thinking, and eliminated many of my prejudices about public education. And contrary to my expectation, the kids I worked with impressed me as a more wholesome, friendly, clear-eyed, all-American bunch than I likely would have worked with at my own academy.

Though my spiritual condition during that time was not particularly strong, I was just enough in tune to see what was going on, even as it was happening. God had deftly turned three bitter disappointments into three outstanding experiences. He really cared about the details of my college life. Those final sixteen months of fury and faith in my college career proved to me that my Heavenly Father really did look out for me in ways beyond my imagination. Even now, when I experience huge disappointments, I think back to those tumultuous days at Atlantic Union College and say to myself: *Keep your chin up. God's probably got something much, much better in mind.* For I know that He "is able to do immeasurably more than all we ask or imagine, according to his power that is at work within us" (Ephesians 3:20, NIV).

There were many people who made this book possible. First, I must acknowledge my wife, Esther, not only for her brilliant idea, but for her constant support, thoughtful criticism, and one particularly stunning piece of business sense that made the whole project financially feasible.

Other members of my family played a great role in the book. My father-in-law, Ramnarine Ramharacksingh, willingly confronted word processing for the first time in his life and entered dozens of stories on computer. At my urgent request, my mother, Rose Marie Knott, just beginning to sample the joys of her recent retirement, willingly plunged back into the fray for a week-and-a-half of long, high-pressure days of data entry, telephone calls, fact checking, corrections, file management, proofreading and general organizing. Alice Ramharacksingh, my mother-in-law, along with Ramnarine, cooked, cleaned, looked after our daughter Olivia, and generally ran our household for several weeks while I was focused on editing and business matters and Esther was occupied at Sligo.

Gil Plubell, director of K-12 education for the North American Division of Seventh-day Adventists, shared my vision for this project. The credibility that his backing lended to my efforts quickly won the interest of other key players and helped them see this was an enterprise worthy of their support. Jerry Thomas, acquisitions editor at Pacific Press, creatively solved a daunting puzzle of complex and even competing goals for the book, and kept it on track. The presidents and other officers of Adventist colleges and universities saw the value of *College Faith* for readers, young and old, in their institutions, and put up the money get it to them. I am grateful for their confidence.

Finally, of course, this book would be nothing without the authors of the stories. The idea of *College Faith* obviously resonated with them, too, as it had with me. I am moved when I consider the scores and scores of church leaders who took the time and significant trouble to write out these stories, often with a remarkable degree of self-disclosure and personal vulnerability. That trait of character inspiring them to share these lessons with others, particularly a younger generation, is probably a good reason why those authors are leaders among us today.

Ronald Alan Knott
Silver Spring, Maryland
September 1995

A BRIDGE TOO NARROW By Bryan Breckenridge

It was Friday noon after another challenging week as a sophomore at Pacific Union College. I was definitely ready for a break. I asked my roommate to take my books back to the dorm so I would waste no time getting down to the Napa Valley on this beautiful day.

I jumped in my 1955 Buick special and drove down the winding mountain road to St. Helena for an afternoon of shopping and lunch. I approached the narrow stone bridge on the east side of town. Two cars ahead were nose to nose on the bridge, and the drivers were yelling at one other to get out of the way.

In the next moment, they were no longer yelling for right of passage but had gotten out of their vehicles and were throwing punches.

Minutes earlier up at the college, I had been sitting in Bob Olson's Bible class. We had discussed God's love for us and how we were to respond to our fellow humans the same way. Before me now were grown men in business suits trying to throw each other off the bridge into the Napa River. Not knowing what else to do, I decided, in my eighteen-year-old wisdom, to jump into the middle and separate these guys.

Thirty years later now as I drive to my office, I travel down Glen Mill Road and cross a nearly identical bridge. I replay the scene that is forever in my memory of two grown men fighting over who was to be first in crossing the bridge. The Glen Mill bridge has three points of access, and as I await my turn, I generally see people who, though busy and anxious to get to their appointments, more often than not reflect their generosity and consideration for one another in the traffic pattern. It reminds me that though the stresses of modern life are great, we still have the responsibility of being respectful of others, "in honour preferring one another."

Back on that narrow bridge outside of St. Helena, I was knocked to the pavement trying to separate the two men in business suits. The shock of seeing a kid lying on the ground brought them to their senses. Immediately civility returned, and apologies were handed around like lollipops.

Each time now as I attend the PUC board of directors meeting I drive over that "Bridge Too Narrow" just to remember one of the more graphic spiritual lessons I learned during my college years.

Be kindly affectioned one to another with brotherly love; in honour preferring one another. Romans 12:10

Bryan Breckenridge is president and chief executive officer of Washington Adventist Hospital in Takoma Park, Maryland, and Shady Grove Adventist Hospital in Rockville, Maryland. He graduated from Pacific Union College in 1968.

BEFORE THEY CALL *By Glenn Aufderhar*

It was exam week, but grades were not the big worry. The letter, on official Walla Walla College stationery, signed by J. Randall Sloope, business manager, made it clear: "No one will be allowed to write final tests without a financial clearance. . . ."

I wearily laid the letter on the night stand. We had known it wouldn't be easy financing my college education after we had a family. But we decided the family was even more important, so my wife remained at home with the children and augmented our income by Tupperware parties and baby-sitting. I had a morning milk delivery route and a job as head sawer at Everett Craik's sawmill in the evening. We met the family's financial needs. We didn't meet my college tuition.

We had sold our new car to finance the first two quarters' tuition. We collected an old debt that covered much of the third quarter. But we still needed $300 cash by morning.

At 4:00 a.m. I got up to study. My wife sleepily whispered, "Why study if you can't take the test?"

Sleeping in sounded good, but I couldn't sleep anyway. Questions plagued my mind: Had we disrupted the family for nothing? Was all the money we had already invested wasted?

I picked up my Bible for morning devotions and continued my journey through Psalms. That morning I read Psalm 78. The power of that chapter made me feel embarrassed that I had questioned God's goodness or His willingness. I asked God for forgiveness for my lack of faith. A sweet peace accompanied my study session for the next two hours.

Suddenly, the morning stillness was broken by a sharp knock. When I opened the door, I found my former employer, Ted Shannon. He had driven through much of the night and arrived at 6:00 a.m. "I don't have time to come in," he said, "but I've been wondering how you are managing financially. Last night I felt impressed to drive by." He thrust some crumpled-up bills in my hand.

Barb came to see what the noise had been. Together we straightened out three $100 bills. I asked her if she had called Esther, Ted's wife. She hadn't. She asked if I had called Ted. I hadn't. "The only thing I did," I said, "was apologize to God for doubting that He would see us through. But by then Ted had already been on the road at least two hours."

Before they call I will answer, while they are yet speaking I will hear. Isaiah 65:24, RSV

Glenn Aufderhar is president of the Adventist Media Center in Simi Valley, California. He graduated from Walla Walla College in 1961.

JUST SAY IT *By Deborah Pontynen Case*

Early-morning phone calls always trigger for me the painful memory of that unexpected call from my parents during my freshman year of college. Arriving back in my dorm room after an early-morning run, my roommate announced I was to immediately call my dad at home.

A lump formed in my throat, and fear filled my heart at the knowledge that something must be terribly wrong. A hundred questions rushed through my head. Each answer held dread.

My sister and I called home at 6:15 that morning. My father told us through broken sobs that our only brother, Bruce, had died in a car accident earlier that morning. The highway patrolman had come to my parents' home at 3:00 a.m. to break the news. They needed to confirm his identity because of the disfiguring nature of Bruce's injuries.

From that point, everything was a blur. Finals were coming up before the summer break, but concerns that had been important just the day before were instantly dismissed. Getting home and being with my parents was all that mattered now. College friends and acquaintances tried to offer condolences, but everything sounded shallow, especially when well-meaning friends said, "I know how you feel." Did they really? Had they lost a handsome, twenty-two-year-old brother who had just entered the prime of life?

I was fortunate to have seen my brother just the previous weekend when he was at college visiting friends. I had told him I loved him very much. My love for Bruce was constant even though he wasn't really living by Adventist standards. He had involved himself in destructive activities such as drinking, which within a few days contributed to his death.

At times I had felt uncomfortable with his behavior and perhaps even been judgmental. But for some reason, when I hugged my brother goodbye on that last visit, our words and actions were loving and accepting. Through this experience, I learned a new life commandment. I was reminded of the proverbs that commend people for bringing joy to others with their words instead of sorrow. And I learned that today is the day kind things are to be spoken to others. Tomorrow may be too late.

The tongue that brings healing is a tree of life . . . and how good is a timely word! Proverbs 15:4, 23, NIV

Deborah Pontynen Case is vice president of Maranatha Volunteers International in Sacramento, California. She graduated from Pacific Union College in 1980.

A RIGHTEOUS CAUSE By G. Ralph Thompson

While I was a student at Caribbean Union College, a new dean of men was installed. He was very strict in enforcing the rules and regulations. Lights were turned off at 10:00 p.m. No noise was to be heard in any room.

Some of the young men in the dormitory felt that the dean was being very legalistic. One night they decided to get even. As soon as the lights went out, they began knocking on the walls and then pounding on anything that would make noise and create a disturbance. The occupants from another room joined in and then another and yet another. It wasn't long before the whole dormitory was resounding with a rising crescendo of cacophony.

The bewildered dean discovered that the noise seemed to be coming from every room. There was laughter and shouting as many students joined in the unusual excitement of flouting the rule that called for quiet.

The dean called the president of the college. By the time he arrived, things began to simmer down, and the dorm became quiet again.

The next day, of course, the faculty met to discuss the little insurrection. They launched an investigation to find the perpetrators. No one came forward with any information about who started the ruckus. So the faculty decided that every student in the men's dormitory had to write several hundred sentences, promising to obey the rules and regulations of the dormitory and the school in general.

I was one of the students in the dormitory. I certainly had not started the ruckus, nor had I pounded on the walls or shouted. But I had laughed and enjoyed the excitement. I searched my conscience to determine whether I should write any sentences, since I hadn't participated in the noise making. I decided that I could not claim complete innocence, since my laughter could have been construed as contributing to, or encouraging, the general noise. So I wrote a few sentences and turned them in.

Three ministerial students in the dormitory insisted that they had not participated in the noise. They refused to write any sentences. The faculty met again to consider their case. They reaffirmed their earlier decision that since no one had come forward to admit to instigating the noise, and it had been general throughout the dormitory, every student would have to write sentences. But the three ministerial students held firm. The faculty threatened them with expulsion for insubordination. At that time, Caribbean Union College was the only real option for anyone from that part of the world wanting to prepare for the Adventist ministry. For these young men, expulsion meant, in effect, the end of their career plans. But they held their ground, and the faculty held theirs.

Tension mounted. Men from the dormitory decided to boycott classes. Women from the other dormitory joined in. An hour's worth of ruckus had turned into a full-blown student strike. The students felt they had a righteous cause. Eventually the board intervened. The three ministerial students were expelled, and the campus gradually returned to normal. None of those three ministerial students ever became ministers.

I have wondered many times since what the future would have been for those three young men had they chosen differently. What might have happened in their lives had they not been so rigid in holding to what they viewed as their righteous cause? Of course, I cannot say for sure.

But it makes me ask if there is ever a time when we should give up our "rights," if necessary, in order to achieve our larger goals? Is there ever a time when the innocent should suffer with the guilty for a larger purpose than proving ourselves right in a particular case?

As students, we go to college to pursue a certain course of study and to finish that course and go on to accomplish our mission in life. Should we be quick to sacrifice that high purpose over a momentary injustice? Should we push as far as expulsion from school and miss the opportunity to accomplish our goals? Should we ever stoop to conquer? What about Jesus' injunction, "If they ask you for your coat, give them your cloak also"?

When those of us who lived through those days in the dormitory meet and reminisce, we all wonder what might have been. How might things have been different if the faculty and board had changed their minds? What might have been different in the lives of the three ministerial students had they decided, in view of their future ambitions, to write the sentences and remain in school?

What would you have done?

If any man will sue thee at the law, and take away thy coat, let him have thy cloak also. And whosoever shall compel thee to go a mile, go with him twain. Matthew 5:40, 41

G. Ralph Thompson is secretary of the General Conference of Seventh-day Adventists in Silver Spring, Maryland. He graduated from Atlantic Union College in 1956.

COLLISION AT THE NAVAL ACADEMY *By Mike Pionkowski*

The true Christian lives in a state of dynamic tension between the goals of God and the goals of the world; between the service of God and the service of the world; between being in the world and not of the world. While we tend to adapt to the tension by avoiding or eliminating circumstances and situations that cause the rub, at times, conflict becomes unavoidable, and we are forced to choose.

As a midshipman at the United States Naval Academy and a growing Christian, my conduct and conscience were dictated by the rules and regulations of the military institution. I never felt any discrepancies or conflicts between the military code of ethics and the Bible until I enrolled in Weapons 101. The course was designed to introduce us to the latest weaponry used in battle. We were taught minute details about the destructive capabilities of the missiles, cannons, and bombs.

During this class, I first felt the collision between military values and those of the Bible. I asked myself if it was possible for a born-again Christian to be involved in wholesale slaughter and mass destruction. When the rule of Caesar and the world conflicted with that of the Bible, what should a Christian do?

I sought counsel from the military chaplains and advice from Christian friends. I diligently studied and prayed. For me, the conflict could only be resolved by resigning my commission and leaving the Naval Academy. It was one of the most difficult life decisions I have ever made; and yet, once I made the decision, I found peace that I had not known for months.

With that decision, my entire life and its direction changed dramatically. As our value systems are being formed and fashioned; as we experience that tension that exists between our Christian conscience and the conduct of the world, may we remember the words of Peter: "We must obey God, not men" (Acts 5:29, TEV).

Then saith he unto them, Render therefore unto Caesar the things which are Caesar's; and unto God the things that are God's. Matthew 22:21

Mike Pionkowski is senior pastor of the Takoma Park Seventh-day Adventist Church in Takoma Park, Maryland. He graduated from Bethany College in 1975.

HE DIDN'T WANT A ROOMMATE *By Jim Greek*

I was awakened from a deep sleep about 2:00 a.m. on a foggy night at Southern College when a heavy green duffle bag hit the floor next to my bed. And then I heard the cutting words "I thought I told that dean I DID NOT WANT A ROOMMATE THIS SEMESTER."

I was a new Adventist. The day before, I had traveled more than four hundred miles to enroll at Southern College. I was eager to start studying for the ministry and enjoy the company of over a thousand students who were ready for translation. Rick's bitter greeting was a rude awakening to reality.

Silence ruled our relationship over the next several days. There were times when I felt like throwing Rick's duffle bag and his attitude out the window. Then it occurred to me that I couldn't really expect to minister in the world if I couldn't even love my roommate.

One day Rick stormed into the room with his usual bad attitude. He was late for work in a nearby city, and his ride just canceled. I tried to bury my head in a book, but my conscience said to me, *"OK, Jim, enough cold warfare. It's time to be like Jesus."* With a gulp in my throat and fear that I would never see my sporty Mercury Cougar again, I slid my keys across the desk without a word. Rick silently took them and left the room.

Around 11:00 p.m., Rick quietly entered the room and crawled into bed. After an long silence, his words floated across the dark room. "I'm sorry I have been a jerk since I arrived. Why did you give me your car anyway?"

The only answer I could come up with was, "Because you are my roommate."

From that moment on, we became best of friends. Several times a day, I would hear the affectionate words "Hey, roomy" from across the campus as we attended our classes. When he introduced me to his friends, it was always, "This is Jim. He's going to be a preach one day."

I discovered that Rick had also been baptized recently. In spite of his rough exterior, he wanted to be like Jesus too. As time progressed, he and I regularly shared what we learned in Bible class. The highlight of our short time together came when he asked if we could pray together. I will never forget the sincerity in his voice and the tears in his eyes. We grew close as we stumbled along together in our new walk with Jesus.

Man looketh on the outward appearance, but the Lord looketh on the heart. 1 Samuel 16:7

Jim Greek is president of the Gulf States Conference of Seventh-day Adventists in Montgomery, Alabama. He graduated from the University of South Florida in 1970.

THREE WISE MEN AND THEIR GIFTS
By Niels-Erik Andreasen

I remember my teachers the best. Most other memories from college days have faded, but the teachers stand out. Here is a testimony to three who left a lasting impression on my life.

The physics teacher who met me after finals on the front steps of the ad building. "What are you going to do when you grow up?" he kidded with his wry smile. "It is a bit vague right now," I admitted. "How about becoming a teacher?" he asked. "Teaching what?" I retorted. "Physics," came his quick reply. "I will not live forever; I need a good successor ready. You could succeed me. Think about it." And he walked away. I did think about it for a long time and decided to make education my lifelong career.

The Bible teacher who walked into class on the first day of the new semester and began asking the names of each of the thirty-five students sitting in front of him. We each responded while he checked our names against his roster, then looked once again at our faces before moving on. That was Monday. Wednesday we returned for the second lecture, but not before our Bible teacher had greeted each one of us by name without the aid of his roster. Our Bible teacher knew us each one by name, on only the second day of the semester! God does too.

The language teacher for whom I was doing a research project as a graduate student. I thought I had got stuck on an insurmountable problem in a difficult text and went to him for advice. "Here is what I have learned so far; what do I do next to solve this problem?" I asked. He listened carefully, then replied that surely by now I had a better understanding of this topic than anyone else on this planet and I ought to use all this information to solve my problem. At first I was disappointed, but soon I realized that my teacher was really not turning me away but rather building up my self-confidence, well enough to solve the problem and publish the results.

Purpose in life, acquaintance with God, and self-confidence—three teachers, three gifts. I am grateful to them for those gifts.

The Lord knows the way of the righteous, but the way of the ungodly shall perish. Psalm 1:6, NKJV

Niels-Erik Andreasen is president of Andrews University in Berrien Springs, Michigan. He graduated from Newbold College in 1963.

THE CALL *By William G. Johnsson*

O ne afternoon in April of my senior year, Ivan Higgins, who was in charge of academic affairs at Avondale College, Australia, asked me to come to his office. There was nothing surprising in that, but he also invited my girlfriend, Noelene Taylor.

Noelene and I were very much in love but not yet engaged. Her father, an Adventist minister, belonged to the old school—I should "prove" myself by a year or two of successful ministerial work after graduation, and only then should I think of asking for Noelene's hand.

Higgins, a great storyteller, began to talk about India. He launched into a long description of a school for missionaries' children some seven thousand feet high in the Himalayas, where everything was either up or down, where the rhododendrons grew wild and turned the mountainside red in the spring and you could look out over the plain and see a hundred miles.

Noelene and I listened and wondered as Higgins went on and on. *Why is he telling us all this? What has this to do with us?*

Higgins paused. Something was coming. He looked us in the eye and said, "You'll be getting a call to that school—you, Bill, to be boys' dean and Bible teacher, and you, Noelene, to teach music."

We were dumbfounded. We had not put in our names for mission service; hadn't even thought about it. Church leaders in Southern Asia had contacted Higgins, an old India hand. Unknown to us, he had given them our names.

Noelene and I left Higgins's office in a daze. We were elated at new and shining prospects, but also confused and uncertain.

The next few months brought greater pressures. Noelene's parents were totally opposed to our marrying and going to India. My church pastor shook his head and warned of getting lost to the work.

As Noelene and I struggled with the call, two inspired statements meant more and more to us. For Noelene, it was Ruth's classic "Where you go I will go, and where you stay I will stay" (Ruth 1:16, NIV). For me, it was these words of Ellen White: "Those who decide to do nothing in any line that will displease God, will know, after presenting their case before Him, just what course to pursue" (*The Desire of Ages*, 668).

We graduated in November (remember, this was "down under"). We married December 21. On January 10 we sailed for India.

"My thoughts are not your thoughts, neither are your ways my ways," declares the Lord. "As the heavens are higher than the earth, so are my ways higher than your ways and my thoughts than your thoughts." Isaiah 55:8, 9, NIV

William G. Johnsson is editor of the Adventist Review *at the General Conference of Seventh-day Adventists in Silver Spring, Maryland. He graduated from Avondale College in 1959.*

WAITING ON THE LORD AND THE COLLEGE PRESIDENT
By L. Stephen Gifford

The matter was settled. There would be no more college for me. I had worked hard all that summer of 1960 as a student literature evangelist, but I had failed. I hadn't earned enough money to pay Southwestern

Junior College what I owed for the last year, let alone the deposit required for the next year.

Then the college president, Lawrence Scales, called me at my home in Louisiana to be sure I was coming back for fall registration.

"No, Elder Scales, I won't be back. I'm going to have to work and forget about a college education. I owe you $785 from last year and have very little money to begin a new school year."

"Well, Steve," his deep voice rumbled, "would you just come over and let us talk with you. At least give us that much." Reluctantly I agreed, but only because I respected Elder Scales so much. I was sure it would be a waste of money to travel from home in Shreveport, Louisiana, over to the college in Keene, Texas.

When I arrived on campus the next morning, I went immediately to the president's office. His secretary said he couldn't see me right then. She sent me to the assistant business manager's office. R. W. Crawford cordially greeted me in his little waiting room and then told me to wait there. An hour went by, and his secretary sent me back to Elder Scales's office. After waiting another hour, it was time for lunch. The secretary gave me a pass to the cafeteria.

At one o'clock, I appeared at Elder Scales's office again and waited another hour. Then I was sent back to Mr. Crawford's office. By now I was disgusted, determined not to wait any longer.

Just then, the jovial director of student finance finally came out of his office and walked me back to Elder Scales's office. This time, I actually got in.

"Steve," Elder Scales began, "I guess you're wondering what's going on."

"Yes, I am. And I'm ready to go back to Shreveport. There isn't any use in my being here, because I don't have any money, and I'm wasting your time and mine."

Elder Scales smiled broadly and carefully intoned, "Yes, there is some use for your trip here. Go to the dorm and unpack your things, because you're staying."

I was thunderstruck. "How can that be?"

"Well, Mr. Crawford and I have been working all morning on the phone, and we have found enough sponsors so that your $800 bill is totally paid. Besides that, we've arranged for you to be an assistant dean in the dormitory, and your college bill will be totally paid!"

Profusely I thanked the two men and walked to the dorm, stunned by God's goodness.

Two overworked educational leaders were not too busy to spend a day on the phone helping a student who had no money. Their caring generosity has been a guidepost to me all through the years. And it reminds me that God works wonderfully in our behalf, but He usually uses human agents to carry out His will.

I'll always feel I owe Elder Scales, Mr. Crawford, and the others a great deal, because they helped me. The least I can do is try to compound their investment by helping others.

Trust in the Lord with all thine heart; and lean not unto thine own understanding. In all thy ways acknowledge him, and he shall direct thy paths. Proverbs 3:5, 6

L. Stephen Gifford is president of the Texas Conference of Seventh-day Adventists in Alvarado, Texas. He graduated from Union College in 1963.

LESSON IN A TV DINNER *By Samuel L. Green*

When I was a student at Southwestern Adventist College, my needs were always greater than the money available. I saved money by living in a small house off campus, and I worked my class schedule around two jobs.

One day, after attending classes and working my first job, I went home to eat before going to my second job. This meal was going to be especially meaningful because it was my last TV dinner and the only food that I had left in the house. And I had no money to buy any more food. It would be my only meal of the day. I was enduring a "forced fast."

The hunger had been gnawing all day, so I relished the blissful anticipation of eating this frozen Mexican dinner. While heating it in the oven, I chanced to scan the ingredients on the packaging. To my dismay, I read that the dinner contained lard.

After some mental wrestling, I decided to be faithful to my convictions and biblical teachings. I threw the dinner into the trash and reminded the Lord of His promise that my "bread and water" would be sure. I drank a large glass of water, put Chap-Stick on my lips to cover their ashen pallor from my hunger, and headed off to work.

When I returned home later that night, I found, to my great joy, a sack containing two large homemade pizzas. The next day, while mentally preparing my angel-of-deliverance testimony, I met the brother of Ben Davis, my friend and fellow theology major. He asked if I had found the pizzas on my doorstep. Ben's wife, Elsie, had made too much pizza dough, which led to extra pizzas, and they decided to give me the two extras.

From this experience, I learned a valuable lesson about being faithful to the Lord's commands at all times, even when it is difficult to obey and when those commands can seemingly be disobeyed in secret.

I also learned how mysteriously the Lord works. Elsie probably never figured out, or even wondered, why she made too much pizza dough. But a faithful Father knew. He had a promise to keep to a faithful child.

O love the Lord, all ye his saints: for the Lord preserveth the faithful, and plentifully rewardeth the proud doer. Psalm 31:23

Samuel L. Green is executive secretary of the Southwestern Union Conference of Seventh-day Adventists in Burleson, Texas. He graduated from Southwestern Adventist College in 1975.

WISDOM AT 1:00 A.M. *By Arthur R. Torres*

I went to college in an era when it was still possible to work one's way through school. So I did. This had the obvious advantage of allowing me to graduate from college debt-free and the hidden disadvantage of having to work so many hours that both my health and my GPA suffered some.

My senior year, because I was saving for graduate school, I worked seventy-two hours a week and carried a full school load. Often I had to study late at night, and I was sometimes overcome by fatigue and literally could not think.

During this period, I discovered a promise that kept both my health and my GPA within the "safe zone."

One night I was writing a paper on "The Theology of Isaiah" for one of my toughest professors. This topic would have been difficult enough for me had I had a well-rested body and mind. But on this particular night, I was so overcome by fatigue that the forty or so texts I had selected as the basis of my paper all seemed to be running together. Try as I might, I could not see the subtleties in the texts or gain a sense of progression for my argument.

I looked down at my typewriter and realized it had been stuck in mid-sentence for more than an hour. Next, I looked at the clock, and it read after 1:00 a.m. I had but nine hours until the paper was due, and I knew that, at the rate I was going, I would never make the deadline.

Suddenly the clouds in my mind cleared, and I remembered a promise from God's Word that I had never claimed. It was James 1:5. I certainly qualified for the promise in that text. I needed wisdom. I dropped to my knees and claimed that promise, but I did not end my prayer without re-

28

minding God that I was stuck, that I needed sleep, and that I knew He was the only One who could help me.

I got up from my knees, and as I did, I saw my paper, in my mind's eye, from start to finish. I saw themes, points, subtleties, progression. I saw an introduction and a conclusion, and I began to type as fast as my fingers would go, and my fingers never stopped flying until I concluded the paper. Incredibly, I did not have to retype it. The first draft became the final draft.

As I finished, I looked at the clock, and it was only 2:30 a.m. I could sleep six hours and make it to class in plenty of time. I dropped to my knees, thanked God for answering my plea, and flopped on the bed without removing my shoes.

That wasn't my last experience with this promise. Often, late at night, when I am struggling with a sermon, I fall on my knees, and I ask God for wisdom, and He has never let me down.

If any of you is lacking in wisdom, ask God, who gives to all generously and ungrudgingly, and it will be given you. James 1:5, NRSV

Arthur R. Torres is senior pastor of Sligo Seventh-day Adventist Church in Takoma Park, Maryland. He graduated from La Sierra University in 1962.

NO MONEY FOR SCHOOL By Marvin Wray

As my wife and I planned to move to Pacific Union College in late 1971, we had a lengthy list of needs. First, we had no money for school. One night, shortly before moving, we were praying, when the phone rang. A member of the local church was calling. He had heard we were leaving and wondered if we had any items for sale. We had just been impressed to sell our color TV/stereo, and when we told him about it, he said that was just the item he wanted. The sale provided exactly the amount of my first quarter's tuition.

So far, so good, but we still had no place to live and no money for rent. Fall quarter was already underway when we arrived on campus. People told us there was no housing available anywhere in the vicinity. I walked through the college market and saw someone put a 3 x 5 card on the bulletin board. It advertised a rental property that had been vacant for six months. The owners, without my saying a word, lowered the rent from $250 to $175. That was exactly the amount we previously had determined we could pay. We paid the rent by selling another household item that, again, we had not advertised in any way. Incidently, the rental was a four-bedroom house on two thousand acres, complete with horses. Our sons didn't seem to mind.

For two full years, God continued to provide our every need financially, physically, spiritually, emotionally, and in every other way. I was a brand-new Christian, weak in faith. It seemed to me God was saying, "You are my child. I will take care of you if you will let Me."

Lord, make me a child again, and help me to trust in Your love.

Don't worry so much about this life—about what to eat or how you look or what you should wear. . . . Stop being so concerned about what to eat and drink. That's what unbelievers worry about. But you have a Father who loves you and knows that you need those things. Luke 12:22-30, The Clear Word

Marvin Wray is ministerial director of the Potomac Conference of Seventh day Adventists in Staunton, Virginia. He graduated from Pacific Union College in 1973.

AUNT NELL *By Robert W. Nixon*

You would've liked my Aunt Nell. She wasn't really a relative, just a neighbor who was a friend of teenagers in Alloway, New Jersey, my hometown.

She was poor but honest, toughened by a life of "takin' in laundry." The last time I visited her, Aunt Nell was sitting in her old oak rocking chair by the kerosene heater, gently wearing the print off the linoleum floor of her kitchen.

As I began to speak, Aunt Nell fumbled with her hearing aid, which promptly fell into one of its screeching fits. Adjustment made, she paused, her blue eyes piercing mine.

"I hear you're takin' law," she said.

She paused again, and then, with a skeptical frown, continued, "Robert, you were such an honest boy."

And that's the challenge Christians face today when society and jobs often ask for compromise.

A wise woman wrote many years ago: "It requires more grace, more discipline of character, to work for God in the capacity of mechanic, merchant, lawyer, or farmer, carrying the precepts of Christianity into the ordinary business of life, than to labor as an acknowledged missionary in the open field. It requires a strong spiritual nerve to bring religion into the workshop and the business office, sanctifying the details of everyday life, and ordering every transaction according to the standard of God's word. But this is what the Lord requires" (*Messages to Young People*, 215, 216).

You must rise to the double challenge: the challenge of career and the challenge of principle. The Lord requires it.

You are the salt of the earth. Matthew 5:13, NIV

Robert W. Nixon is general counsel to the General Conference of Seventh-day Adventists in Silver Spring, Maryland. He graduated from Columbia Union College in 1961.

JUST SAY "NO" *By Leslie Bumgardner*

I remember the Saturday night well. It was the end of spring quarter, and the final project for my Art in Everyday Living class was due first thing Sunday morning. Our instructor had already extended the deadline, so I knew it would be futile to ask for another extension. And here I was, with three other class members, frantically working to complete the project. A house plan, carpet and fabric samples, and pictures of home furnishings were strewn about on the floor of our dining room.

In fairness to the instructor, I must confess that the project had been announced at the beginning of the course, and she had been urging us to be sure and pace ourselves so we wouldn't be caught short at the end of the quarter. And while I had worked for short spurts of time on it earlier in the quarter, I now found myself with hours of work yet to do and, it seemed, even fewer hours in which to do it!

My fellow classmates found themselves in the same predicament and so we banded together for moral support with plans to work through the night. After an occasional cat nap, I found myself completing my project as the sun began to rise. With the finishing touches in place, I raced to my instructor's office and wearily left the project with her.

As I reflected on the all-too-numerous occasions in which I found myself up against a deadline, I learned a lesson I continue to relearn today. If I am to minimize the needless stress from being overwhelmed by deadlines and unfinished projects, I must learn to say "No" to activities and requests that distract me from my final goals. And in order to see clearly what are distractions and what enhances my progress to my goal, I must keep my relationship with God in balance through Bible study and prayer.

This one thing I do: forgetting what lies behind and straining for-

ward to what lies ahead, I press on toward the goal for the prize of the heavenly call of God in Christ Jesus. Philippians 4:13, 14, NRSV

Leslie Bumgardner is associate pastor of the Walla Walla College Church in College Place, Washington. She graduated from Walla Walla College in 1975.

NO ONE UNDERSTANDS LIKE JESUS By Benjamin F. Reaves

Someone ran down the hallway toward my room in Irwin Hall, the men's dormitory at Oakwood College. The knock was rapid and the voice loud and insistent.

"Reaves—Benny Reaves!! Phone call, long-distance call in the lobby."

I rolled off my top bunk, stumbled out of my room, and ran down the steps to the phone booth in the lobby. As I blurted out "hello," I heard the voice of my mother. In a strained, halting voice, her few words turned my world upside down: "Daddy has died."

"When? How? Where?" Bit by bit I heard of his sudden, brief hospitalization and unexpected death from an aneurysm.

On that small campus, the word traveled like wildfire. The next morning it seemed as if everyone knew about it. Everywhere I went, almost everyone I passed spoke what were meant to be words of comfort. To me, their words were like battering rams that repeatedly smashed at the wall of emotional control I tried desperately to maintain.

It became so difficult to maintain my self-control I soon wished that everyone would stop saying, "I'm sorry you lost your dad." *Just stop talking about it!* In my disorientation, it seemed as if they were just being polite.

As I walked from Moran Hall past the Bell Tower, with my head down, trying to avoid eye contact, someone walking by touched me on the arm. I looked up and saw the face of a friend from my home church—a friend who had lost her father the year before. All she said was, "Benny, I understand."

Her words embraced my emotions. I found a comfort that other expressions of sympathy were not able to give. She was not saying polite, appropriate, well-meaning words. She *knew* my pain. She knew my tears that would not be blinked back; the permanent change in my world. She understood.

As I started up the steep steps of Irwin Hall, an incredibly powerful comfort filled my soul. Not only did my friend know my pain, but my Friend knew too.

> No one understands like Jesus,
> When the days are dark and grim.
> No one is so near, so dear as Jesus.
> Cast your every care on Him.

We have not an high priest which cannot be touched with the feeling of our infirmities. Hebrews 4:15

Benjamin F. Reaves is president of Oakwood College in Huntsville, Alabama. He graduated from the same institution in 1955.

THE POWER OF A DREAM *By Tim Crosby*

When I was a theology student at Southern College, I had a dream. That dream was to preach at the 11:00 Sabbath-morning service in the Collegedale Church before I graduated from college. I don't remember when it first began to take definite shape. I don't remember ever telling anyone about that dream, but I rehearsed it many times in my mind. I imagined myself standing behind that heavy wooden pulpit, speaking authoritatively to a congregation that was taking in every word. A sea of faces looked up at me in rapt attention, their silence broken only by an occasional cough. I rehearsed my action and their reaction with no clue as to what I was actually saying. Thirty, forty, perhaps fifty times I reran that mental videotape in living Technicolor.

One day in my senior year, the pastor of the church, Elder Gary Patterson, invited me into his office and stunned me with an invitation to preach at the Sabbath-morning service.

Oh, joy! What an honor! How I thanked God and how I prayed and prepared. Finally the day came, and I stood in the pulpit, gazing at a sea of faces looking up at me in rapt attention, their silence broken only by an occasional cough.

When it was over, Elder Patterson remarked that he thought it was one of the five best sermons he had heard preached from that pulpit, and, to my chagrin, corrected my mispronunciation of the word *secreted*.

Before graduating, I preached a second time when I was asked to take the Sabbath service at a student-led Week of Prayer.

I learned two things from this: the power of a vision and the delight of being on the receiving end of grace. Gary Patterson was willing to give up his pulpit and take a risk on a novice, and I have never forgotten.

A few years later, while pastoring a church in northern Georgia, I ran into Steve. He was a former fellow seminarian who had become discouraged and was not living up to his convictions. I invited him to church and eventually asked him to fill the pulpit for me one Sabbath—over the objections of an elder. That invitation marked a turning point in his life. Today, Steve is a faithful pastor.

OK, Steve, now it's your turn.

Each of you should look not only to your own interests, but also to the interests of others. Philippians 2:4, NIV

Tim Crosby is acquisitions editor at the Review and Herald Publishing Association in Hagerstown, Maryland. He graduated from Southern College in 1977.

TEN DESPERATE DAYS By Floyd M. Murdoch

Somehow, I had managed to keep track of the days, and this was Sabbath. And it was *one* Sabbath I shall never forget. It was the 3rd of July, 1965.

We were lost, terribly and hopelessly lost, somewhere in the jungles of eastern Peru. There were no villages, no roads, not even an Indian from whom to ask directions. Occasionally we would see a small plane that appeared to be looking for us, but we were certain they could not see our frantic waving under the dense foliage.

Two weeks earlier, our biological expedition had started out in high spirits for a two- to three-day "downhill jaunt" along the jungle trails toward the Nevati River, where dugouts awaited us for a four-hour trip downstream to the mission landing strip. In the beginning, our group consisted of twelve biologists, ten Campa porters, and two native guides under the leadership of Doctors Asa Thoresen and Don Seidel of Andrews University. Once it became evident we were lost, the porters, and what little food was left, vanished into the jungle. Only one guide remained, and he was obviously lost.

Now it was Sabbath. We had been in the jungle for thirteen days. The rain had finally stopped. Even though I had eaten very little over the preceding ten desperate days, the warmth and light from the sun made the jungle come alive. My courage renewed. I became sure we would make it. Several of my colleagues were sure we would not. One friend was experiencing convulsions while others were having fainting spells. One member even threw his belongings over the cliff, thinking he would die before nightfall. Like the Children of Israel, many of the group criticized our leader, Dr. Thoresen, but he never lost his cheerful spirit and always tried to encourage us.

Often on the trails I found myself discouraged. When I fell down, it was difficult to get up. Too weak to sing and walk, I found humming hymns to myself seemed to make the jungle ridges less steep. Then came Sabbath. I decided to leave my pack behind and strike out to find help. As I struggled, somewhat oblivious to my surroundings, the *moo* of a cow did not seem significant. Then all at once the *moo* hit me like an electric shock. Where there is a cow, there must be a farm. I yelled and yelled, but no one answered. I stumbled downhill through the jungle toward the cow. A fence! A barn! Beyond that, a cluster of several houses. Soon all my fellow wanderers were inside eating oranges, tomatoes, bananas, and bread. We had not waited for an invitation. The houses were empty. No one was home. Where were they? Had angels prepared our feast? I'm not sure who was more surprised, the villagers who returned to find us in their homes or our group members to find that after wandering for two weeks in the jungle, we had, incredibly, stumbled into an *Adventist* village while all the community had been in church. Except for that cow, we might still be lost. We had been "saved" by a one-word "sermon" from the Sabbath people's cow— *moo.*

The Son of Man has come to seek and to save that which was lost. Luke 19:10, NKJV

Floyd M. Murdoch is director of governmental relations for the Adventist Development and Relief Agency, International, in Silver Spring, Maryland. He graduated from Andrews University in 1964.

SILLY LITTLE PRANKS
AND A STILL, SMALL VOICE *By Rosa Taylor Banks*

I probably had more roommates than any college student should have: five—and that was during just two years at one college. I remember my fifth roommate most affectionately, because unlike all the others, she and I were kindred spirits.

Ruth and I were different in many ways, but in temperament we were almost exactly the same. That is why we got along so well and why we got into so much trouble too. It wasn't the kind of trouble that earned us serious punishment. We just loved to pull pranks on other students. And we were the kind who dared to challenge rules we deemed unfair. The "system" was always our favorite target.

We got away with many little pranks. We taped signs on people's doors about changes in daily schedules. We sent out "official" memos to students to come pick up yearbooks when the administrative office was not ready to hand them out. Such "little things" brought much excitement to what we felt was an otherwise small and boring campus. But deep within, we knew that even these seemingly "little things" were wrong. If we were truly bored, there were other, more profitable avenues for upgrading the campus social program. We were also aware that if we kept this behavior up, it would only spell trouble for us down the road. And so the Holy Spirit continued to work on us in spite of ourselves.

On one pivotal occasion, we were tempted to "break" a serious rule. One of our friends had overstayed her curfew and phoned us to open the side entrance to the dorm so she could get in. We actually went up to the door a few times. But that still, small voice tugging at our hearts just wouldn't let us open the door.

We learned later that the dean had been tipped off. Anyone who touched that door would set off an alarm that would put them on a bus for home the next day.

After this experience, Ruth and I settled down. Our days of pulling pranks and breaking rules were over. We actually grew up that night from two playful, silly-acting girls to maturing young college women. We still praise the Lord to this day that His Spirit steered us away from a split-second act that may have altered our college experience and the course of our lives for years.

Good and upright is the Lord; therefore he instructs sinners in the way. Psalm 25:8, RSV

Rosa Taylor Banks is director of the Office of Human Relations and associate secretary of the North American Division of Seventh-day Adventists in Silver Spring, Maryland. She graduated from Oakwood College in 1967.

GOD'S NUDGE *By Bruce Johnston*

"Why did I ever come to college?" I asked myself as I wrestled with bulletins, class schedules, and registration forms, *ad infinitum*. Enrolling two weeks late hadn't helped the frustration level. There were no registration counselors sitting behind tables in the gym to answer a myriad of questions. Fortunately, at that moment, I began to reflect on the events that led me to Walla Walla College. I realized that I was there because God obviously nudged me in that direction.

It may have started when a college recruiter visited my friend. When my friend told him that I had just completed high school, the recruiter gave me a pitch that left me unimpressed, or so I thought. Though I had no plans that included college, that recruiter must have planted a seed that germinated ever so slowly through the summer. The summer was over and college had already begun when I felt strongly convicted that I should sell my car and go. Selling the car took more than a week.

When I told my friend that I was going to hitchhike on Sunday from Medford up through Portland and over to Walla Walla, he replied, "I'll go with you as far as Portland and get a job there." Sunday, at 7:00 a.m., we stood at the junction of Highways 60 and 99 in Medford, Oregon. Two fruitless hours later, the Big V Market opened, and my friend said, "I don't think we're ever going to get a ride. I'm going to see if I can get a job here." He did and worked there for two years.

At 5:00 p.m. I was in Grants Pass, a whole thirty miles closer to Walla Walla. "My friend is right about getting a ride," I said to myself. Striding to the other side of the highway, I stuck out my thumb and immediately got a ride back to Medford. So much for college.

Mr. Babcock, who owned a service station where teenagers often hung around working on their cars, looked up in surprise when I walked in.

"You're supposed to be at Walla Walla," he chided.

"I tried all day, but I don't think God wants me to go."

"Oh yes He does, and tomorrow I'm taking you there myself." This man, who had only an elementary education himself, must have seen something in me I didn't see. He hired someone to pump gas, and the next day we were off to College Place, 450 miles away. Mr. Babcock returned home the same day. You can figure how much sleep he got that night.

God apparently had impressed this man to think about my problem. Mr. Babcock, in turn, gave me a nudge at one of those crucial moments in personal history when decisions are made that so greatly influence the course of life and service for God.

I will instruct you and teach you in the way you should go; I will counsel you and watch over you. Psalm 32:8, NIV

Bruce Johnston is president of the North Pacific Union Conference of Seventh-day Adventists in Portland, Oregon, and chairman of the board of Walla Walla College. He graduated from Walla Walla College in 1950.

RESCUE ON THE MOUNTAIN *By Milton R. Siepman*

One beautiful holiday morning at Helderberg College in South Africa, a group of students had decided to climb the mountain behind the school. On their way up the face of the precipitous slope, their leader, Percy Mew, stood on a huge boulder to watch the group climbing below him. Suddenly the boulder began to move. Although he jumped aside, it broke loose from its base and began to roll toward the climbers. He watched with horror as it hit Corrie Britton and hurled him aside. It brushed by several girls and fell squarely on Jose Rodriguez's foot, severing a big toe, before rumbling into the valley below.

Percy ran back down to the college to get help and arrange for ambulances to come up the mountain road to a point closest to the scene of the accident. Several of us who were working on the farm that day volunteered to help. Grabbing first-aid equipment and stretchers to carry the injured, we rushed up the steep slope to render what aid we could.

Three casualties needed to be carried to the waiting ambulances, and only six of us were available to do so. In order to keep the stretchers reasonably level down the steep and rocky slope, the bearer in front carried the handles on his shoulders while the bearer at the rear carried the stretcher at arm's length, stooping as low as possible.

John Coetzee and I carried Jose that day. Since he weighed about two hundred pounds and I had the rear position at the stretcher, the burden rapidly became almost unbearable. The stooped position, the constant weight on the arms, the stress on the shoulders, together with the steep, rocky terrain, made every step one of sheer agony. But we dared not stop.

Then someone began to sing a song made famous by George Beverly Shea. The strains of "He Carried My Burden to Calvary" began to echo down the mountain. As we joined in and sang together, the burdens we carried somehow became lighter. We began to have a sense of the burden Christ had carried for us, without complaint, as He staggered and stumbled to the top of His hill. As we recognized the enormity of the sin burden He carried for us, our burdens seemed smaller, and we moved ahead with a tangible appreciation for what He had done for us.

He carried my burden and yours.

Surely he hath borne our griefs, and carried our sorrows: yet we did esteem him stricken, smitten of God, and afflicted. Isaiah 53:4

Milton R. Siepman is president of Tennessee Christian Medical Center in Nashville, Tennessee. He graduated from Helderberg College in 1957.

WHO CAN YOU TRUST? By Jere D. Patzer

Some of my college friends and I decided we wanted to do something unprecedented for the Lord and the community. So during my junior year we planned a full-blown evangelistic crusade right in the College Church.

As in any academic setting, our idea was not universally acclaimed; but in general, people warmed to the idea. We made our plans, hired an evangelist, sent out advertising, and prayed. As a campus student leader, and the one responsible for the crusade, I invested tremendous emotional and physical energy in ensuring its success.

By the week before the crusade was to start, we had everything ready. And then a terrible thing happened. The college president called me to his office and solemnly explained that our evangelist wouldn't be conducting the meetings. The president said that the evangelist had just left his wife and skipped town with another woman.

I was stunned, devastated. How could this respected leader among God's people do such a thing? I, a young preacher-to-be, had looked up to him and put such great faith in his leadership. It was unthinkable that such a thing could happen.

On very short notice, we found another evangelist, and he conducted a successful series. But the lessons I learned through this bitter disappointment—lessons learned through tears of frustration and anger—have stayed with me.

First, I learned that God is not dependent on any of us to accomplish His plans. Second, I learned that we must not put inordinate faith in people, for even the brightest lights will sometimes go out.

Many years later, I remember those college lessons much more clearly than many I was taught from textbooks.

It is better to trust in the Lord than to put confidence in man. Psalm 118:8, NKJV

Jere D. Patzer is president of the Upper Columbia Conference of Seventh-day Adventists in Spokane, Washington. He graduated from Atlantic Union College in 1969.

GOD WORKS IN TIME! *By Theodore T. Jones II*

I had neither a big savings account nor monied parents. But I did have an unpaid account with the college, with final exams approaching. That meant no exams. I didn't know what to do, so I just went about my job at the campus print shop. I was convinced that somehow, God would either plead my case effectively with the business office or, just maybe, do something unusual for me.

Just before final exams were to begin, I walked out of Irwin Hall, the men's dorm, en route to the administration building. Elder Robert Woodfork, the dean of men, intercepted me on the sidewalk.

"Brother Ted," he said, "somebody must really like you out in Kansas, because they have sent something to the college to help you!" He brandished a slip of paper showing that $250 had been applied to my account by an anonymous donor.

Being quick of eye, I saw an embossed address on the envelope before Dean Woodfork could put the papers back into his suit pocket. The address belonged to a Christian family in my hometown of Hutchinson, Kansas. They owned a large crafts business. My mother worked for their company.

The Ericksons' kindness and surprise gift enabled me to take my finals! What they gave was more than I needed and came just at the right time.

Two years later, I was thrilled to visit the Ericksons and thank them for their timely gift. I was even happier when they consented to let me pray with them for their continued success in business. This is one soul who returned to give thanks!

When the Holy Spirit sends someone to me in need of help and encouragement, I remember the many times others lifted my load and gave me assistance.

It shall come to pass, that before they call, I will answer; and while they are yet speaking, I will hear. Isaiah 65:24

Theodore T. Jones II is president of the Atlantic Union Conference of Seventh-day Adventists in South Lancaster, Massachusetts, and chairman of the board of Atlantic Union College. He graduated from Oakwood College in 1956.

REASON, REGURGITATION, AND PERFECTION *By Jim Brauer*

I have always wrestled with the human frailty that somehow I must be perfect. I cannot simply be adequate or average. I cannot allow that I may have made a mistake; I must be *perfect*.

During my freshman year, I sat in a world history class with a paper in front of me that I could not believe. The grade on it suggested that I was less than perfect. In fact, it was so far less than perfect that tears welled up at the edges of my eyes. This simply could not be. How could I have gotten such a grade? I had dutifully and faithfully regurgitated everything I had been taught. How dare somebody give me an average grade for doing what I was supposed to do! I decided that I must figure this teacher out, redeem my wounded pride, and continue on in my illusion of perfection.

So, I set out to study this teacher, Cedric Ward, and to try to understand just what he wanted from me. But the weeks rolled by, and I didn't make any progress. My frustration grew. Apparently, he didn't want his notes faithfully transcribed.

At last, it dawned on me that he wanted me to think. Unfortunately, I hadn't been trained to think. Yes, I could spot the hidden, tricky question that would determine the difference between those of us who were perfect and those who were merely average. But this teacher wanted me to think. And the scariest part was that when I thought, I wasn't all that impressed with what I thought. My thinking seemed merely average. And even more scary was the realization that if my thoughts were average, just maybe I was average too. And if I were average, then I wasn't perfect. Perfect is never average.

Thinking is a dangerous thing. It forces you to examine your priorities, your presuppositions. It is so much easier not to think. It is so much easier not to examine why. *Just tell me the right answer. Just give me a good grade. Let me move on. Let me go become a pastor and regurgitate all the right an-*

swers. But don't make me think.

Cedric Ward became my favorite teacher, as I confronted my imperfection and the realization that I didn't have to be perfect. He helped me discover that it was, in fact, fun to think and explore, to ask hard questions. But it was also painful.

The lesson of having to think remains with me even now. It requires that I continually fight the urge to conform to what everyone else says. It forces me to keep asking questions and challenging. It inspires me to create an environment in which I enable other people—pastors and teachers—to think, so that each of us will one day sit down with God and reason together.

Come now, and let us reason together, saith the Lord: though your sins be as scarlet, they shall be as white as snow; though they be red like crimson, they shall be as wool. Isaiah 1:18

Jim Brauer is president of the Rocky Mountain Conference of Seventh-day Adventists in Denver, Colorado. He graduated from Union College in 1974.

THEY RESPECTED MY CHOICES *By Marit Balk*

There were no Adventist colleges in my country when I grew up, so I had to go to a public college. Since I had already gone to public school all my life, it was really nothing new, except that this time the college was in Amsterdam and not in my hometown. Every day I walked ten minutes to the train station, sat twenty minutes on the train, and ended the trip with a twenty-minute bus ride.

The major I chose was mainly of interest to women, but we had a few guys in our class, though most of them dropped out during or after the first year. I enjoyed school, liked the teachers, and even liked my fellow students; it was just during break time that life got really tough.

In Holland, it rains a fair amount of the time. We stayed inside most of the time during break, which was fine, except that it seemed like everybody smoked! And that was not the only thing. After school, especially on Fridays, most girls went to cafes or bars to get something to drink. That "something" contained alcohol. Twenty years ago, to say that you didn't drink was not the "cool" thing to do. Most parties and class activities took place on Friday nights during Sabbath hours. Sometimes the parties were at somebody's apartment and sometimes at school. I stood out like a sore thumb. I was not particularly popular; I didn't smoke, drink, dance, or party on Friday nights. And I told my classmates why. They had a hard time understanding, but they kept asking. Fortunately, I was involved in a fun youth group and was very active in Pathfinders in my church. And frankly, I didn't need to participate in my classmates' parties. I think this intrigued them, and they asked more questions. What else could I do but share with them my life as a child of God?

I am not sure how it all happened, but my classmates started to organize parties after sundown on Saturday nights. They always had something non-alcoholic to drink, and they didn't laugh at me if I didn't want to go with them to the disco. They respected me and my choices! I will never forget my four years at a public college. I continue to pray that I will keep my courage and stand up for what I believe.

Be strong and courageous. Do not be afraid or terrified because of them, for the Lord your God goes with you; He will never leave you nor forsake you. Deuteronomy 31:6, NIV

Marit Balk is assistant pastor of Pacific Union College Church in Angwin, California. She graduated from De Noord Hollandse Scholengemeenschap in 1980.

MY 1943 PLODGE *By Malcolm Maxwell*

When I was in college, I drove a 1943 Plodge. A 1943 what? A Plodge. You have never heard of such a car? I'm not surprised, for it was one of a kind—a 1937 Plymouth business coupe with a 1947 Dodge engine, hence a 1943 Plodge.

Although already old and well-used when I bought it from an older brother, the car was in great shape and was one of the joys of my life when I was a student at Pacific Union College in the 1950s.

This two-seater opened up a whole new world of opportunity for fun and friends. It also allowed me to take employment that would have been impossible without wheels, and I needed additional income—cars are expensive.

My primary job was on the campus grounds crew, but all the money I made went toward my school bill. If I needed cash, I had to earn it elsewhere. And with my Plodge, I could. It allowed me to take a job off campus running an eighty-pound air hammer digging ditches for a water company nearby. The work was hard but paid well—and in cash!

Perhaps what I liked best about my car was the sense of freedom and empowerment it gave me. I could pretty much come and go as I pleased as long as there was gas in the tank. But here is an important lesson: freedom can be lost.

As much as I loved my Plodge, it did have its idiosyncrasies, including an erratic gas gauge. Sometimes the gauge told the truth, and sometimes it didn't! Late one dark night in a lonely stretch of countryside on my way home from PUC, my motor died. I was out of gas and out of freedom—stuck by the side of the road until someone came to my rescue.

Freedom is like that. It is precious but vulnerable and must be protected. It is a gift but can be lost. God created human beings free so we can choose to love and serve each other. Through sin, our freedom was lost, and we became slaves until Christ won it back again. Now He calls us to freedom (see Galatians 5:13) and counsels us to "stand firm" in this new liberty He has gained for us at such cost and "refuse to be tied to the yoke of slavery again" (Galatians 5:1, NEB).

For freedom Christ has set us free; stand fast therefore, and do not submit again to a yoke of slavery. Galatians 5:1, RSV

Malcolm Maxwell is president of Pacific Union College in Angwin, California. He graduated from the same institution in 1956.

A BAG OF PENNIES AND AN EMPTY CUPBOARD *By Thomas R. Neslund*

It was Thirteenth Sabbath. In our home, and in our college life, that meant it was time to square up all our financial covenants with the Lord.

That might be a fine thing to do if one was experiencing normal college life, but ours had been a little abnormal lately. My wife was confined to bed rest in an effort to bring her first pregnancy to term. The kitchen cupboards were empty. I was in school on the GI Bill, and the government was three months behind in sending my checks.

Our refrigerator held half a loaf of bread and about two glasses of orange juice. I badly needed a haircut. We had only a dollar and a half in the house—if we didn't count the bag of pennies we had been saving for many weeks and had pledged to give for the Thirteenth Sabbath investment offering.

What should we do? Certainly the Lord would understand our extremity. Surely He would temporarily release us from our commitment.

My wife and I talked about our problem, and then we decided to honor our commitment. We wouldn't use the bag of pennies to buy groceries. We would turn it in for the investment offering as pledged. I took the bag of pennies to the local market to have it changed to four one-dollar bills and larger denominations of coins.

As I stood in line, I wondered what would happen when we were totally broke. How would we get through the weekend? When my turn came at the register, I told the clerk that I had 480 pennies. Would she kindly give me four ones and eighty cents in coin?

"I'm sorry," she said. "I'll have to count them first."

Someone in the line behind me muttered: "I would have to get behind someone like you!" Embarrassed for the trouble I was making, I told the clerk, "I'm going next door to get a haircut, and I'll be back in a half-hour or so." She said she would have my money ready.

After the haircut, and now down to the last quarter of our own money, I collected the investment-offering money from the clerk. That evening, I went to the vesper service, where the offering would be collected. With a sense of great meaning, I put our $4.80 into the basket as it passed my pew.

When I returned home after the meeting, I was stunned to find four large boxes of groceries on our doorstep. I couldn't believe my eyes. It was show-and-tell time! My wife was speechless as I fixed dinner. All we could say was, "Where? Who? How?"

The next morning when I returned home after church, I found three more boxes of food. And we found even more boxes at the close of that incredible Sabbath. Our refrigerator and cupboards were filled to capacity; we stacked food on the countertops and on the floor.

We never learned where all that food came from. All we know is that God had kept His famous promise in an astounding and literal way.

Bring ye all the tithes into the storehouse, that there may be meat in mine house, and prove me now herewith, saith the Lord of hosts, if I will not open you the windows of heaven, and pour you out a blessing, that there shall not be room enough to receive it. Malachi 3:10

Thomas R. Neslund is executive director of the International Commission for the Prevention of Alcoholism and Drug Dependency, at the the General Conference of Seventh-day Adventists in Silver Spring, Maryland. He graduated from Union College in 1964.

CAUGHT RED-HANDED *By George R. Knight*

A door slammed. As the echoes reverberated through what I thought was an empty women's dorm, I broke into a cold sweat. A few seconds later, my worst fears were confirmed.

There I stood, face to face with the prototype of the ultraprotective women's dean—Evabelle Winning. This slim, severe-looking little woman knew how to make her point. And she had me this time.

Why was a male student prowling around in the lobby of a locked women's dormitory during the holiday season? How did I get in? What mischief was I up to?

Within seconds, she landed on me with all fours, and I had nowhere to escape. She had caught me red-handed and was making the most of it.

Few times in my life have I been the target of such a verbal tirade of righteous indignation from an authority figure. She had me. She had no intention of showing the slightest mercy.

What Miss Winning didn't know was that her associate dean had let me in and had told me to wait in the lobby while she went to one of the women's rooms to get a book I desperately needed.

My first thought was to defend myself from the unjust onslaught. From the look on the dean's face and the sound of her voice, I instinctively knew that such a course would only raise her heat and intensity.

That very morning I had been reading Dale Carnegie's bestseller *How to Win Friends and Influence People*. Carnegie said that when one faced this very type of attack, the best thing to do is not to argue. I should profusely confess how sorry and wrong I was and tell the other person that I deserved just what I was getting. That would result, he maintained, in the other person coming over to my side and saying it wasn't as bad as I thought it was.

Against my natural instincts, I followed Carnegie's advice. That took the good dean by surprise, since she expected resistance. In a few seconds, she was seeking to comfort me.

That left an opening for us to work out the truth. By the time the associate returned, we had solved the problem and were even having a pleasant conversation.

A soft answer turns away wrath, but a harsh word stirs up anger. Proverbs 15:1, RSV

George. R. Knight is professor of church history at the Seventh-day Adventist Theological Seminary at Andrews University in Berrien Springs, Michigan. He graduated from Pacific Union College in 1965.

THE DOORS OF FAITH *By Gene C. Milton*

My college days were the turning point in my life. It was not that I had it so bad before college, but the things I have accomplished and the blessings I received during and after college have been far beyond any expectations or personal goals I ever dreamed. The real turning point was my decision to leave a good-paying job and ask my wife of one year to put our trust and faith in the Lord and move five hundred miles away to a strange place to attend a Christian college.

Our young pastor encouraged us to pray that the Lord would open and shut doors to show us the way He would have us go. The pastor said we should then proceed in faith. If the path opened before us, we shouldn't question the evidence, but trust in God's promises and move forward. And that's what we did.

Those college days were the best of our married life. We didn't have much, but we met wonderful friends who were in the same position and have remained our friends throughout the years.

We arrived at college with no idea of what it would cost, financially or physically, to get my college degree. Yet, without financial help from anyone, I was able to graduate with my bill paid in full as well as have enough money to put down on a new car to move us to my business internship in California.

None of this would have been possible without complete trust and reliance upon the Lord. He provided for our every need without our having to calculate and figure out every step on our own. This doesn't mean we didn't have to work hard. We did. But the Lord provided us with work opportunities to meet every need.

Throughout my professional career, I have continued to use the same principle of praying to God to open and close doors and then to move forward in faith. Every job that I have been offered has made me wonder if I was capable of handling it. Everyone else has seemed to know so much more than I. As I pray and move forward in faith, I am amazed at how God continues to bless someone like me, who without God can do nothing. But *with* God there isn't anything I can't do!

Do you see that faith was working together with his works, and by works faith was made perfect? James 2:22, The New Open Bible

---

Gene C. Milton is president and chief executive officer of Hackettstown Community Hospital in Hackettstown, New Jersey. He graduated from Atlantic Union College in 1972.

EAGER EVANGELIST, RELUCTANT TEACHER
By Werner Vyhmeister

It was almost the end of the summer vacation. I was getting ready to take the last two semesters of my five-year "Profesorado" in history and geography at the University of Chile in Santiago. And then the phone rang.

Dr. Alcides J. Alva, acting president of Chile College, the Adventist school in Chillan, was calling. Five teachers had left, including the president. They urgently needed faculty replacements. Would I consider teaching, at least for one year, beginning in three weeks?

The call took me totally by surprise. Four years before I had graduated from the two-year ministerial program at Chile College. I wanted to be an evangelist. But at eighteen I sensed that I needed to gain both in years and knowledge before I could work full time for the church. So I had enrolled in the University of Chile. For the next four years, I pastored part time while studying at Santiago. During those years, I had been involved in several successful evangelistic series. I was the leader of a group of Adventist university students in Santiago, and we had conducted some of the campaigns. It was very good experience for my intended life work. Dr. Alva's request was very troubling. Why should I drop my professional goals of becoming an evangelist to go and teach at the college?

The next day I met Dr. Alva at a train junction near my hometown. We talked for about twenty minutes before his train left. With kindness and clarity, backed by his own life experience, he gave answers to my objections. I wasn't convinced, but I promised to pray about it.

While I stood on the platform waiting for my train, I prayed about my problem. Suddenly my mind made a 180-degree turn. It started generating answers to problems that had puzzled me just moments before. The tension and misgivings about delaying my studies for one year gave way to a sense of inner joy that was difficult to explain.

Teaching church history, Biblical archaeology, and other courses at Chile College during the 1954 school year was a most rewarding experience. At the end of the year, I knew that I wanted to invest my life in preparing ministers through teaching. Forty years later, I look back with gratitude to my heavenly Father for stepping unexpectedly into my life and reorienting my professional goals.

Commit your way to the Lord; trust in him, and he will act. Psalm 37:5, NRSV

Werner Vyhmeister is dean of the Seventh-day Adventist Theological Seminary at Andrews University in Berrien Springs Michigan. He graduated from the University of Chile in 1956.

THE BIG PICTURE *By Doug Kilcher*

I didn't work for the dean of men, so when he called me into his office, I knew I was in trouble. I was a freshman at an Adventist college on the West Coast. It was a tumultuous year for me: my first time away from home to explore new freedom; a chance to engage in any immature behavior I could get away with.

There certainly had been trouble. The dean described the incident and asked if I knew anything about it. "Oh no, nothing at all," I said confidently. He gave a reluctant sigh and put away his papers.

"That will be all for now," he said. "You may go."

Several days passed, and I was again called down to the dean's office. This time a policeofficer stood beside the dean. The dean looked me directly in the eye and said, "This gentleman wants to ask you some questions."

This time I faced the relentless, peering eyes of two authority figures, and I knew the game was over.

"Yes, sir. I was there. I participated."

The next day, I was one of three students who cleared out their rooms and went home with some very disappointed parents. It was a long, unhappy trip, filled with lectures and dire predictions of what would happen if I didn't get my life straightened out and didn't learn from this experience.

Later, the college decided to take one of us back the following year. They also arranged for the other two to attend a different college to complete their education. At the time, we were highly critical of the harsh decision. Now I see that it was the best thing for all of us. The discipline meted out at that pivotal moment in our lives helped to shape all three of us into successful, contributing citizens.

I deserved what I received. I learned to speak the truth. I learned to take the punishment. Then I put it behind me and lived above it. I had to pay a high price, but I never again participated in a reckless prank that could hurt or embarrass anyone.

I *can* rise when I fall. Disgrace and humiliation can sometimes, in the big picture, be a good thing. It can cause us to look up and to reach out to the only One who can really help us grow and learn from difficult experiences.

Do not rejoice against me, O my enemy, for though I fall, I will rise again! When I sit in darkness, the Lord himself will by my Light. Micah 7:8, TLB

Doug Kilcher is associate professor of Christian ministry at the Seventh-day Adventist Theological Seminary at Andrews University in Berrien Springs, Michigan. He graduated from La Sierra University in 1967.

YOUR WORK WILL BE REWARDED

By B. Lyn Behrens

The day for my year-end Neuroanatomy exam had dawned. I had slept fitfully—sleep interrupted by confusing dreams of neuronal pathways and networks. Stress was maximal. There would not be a second chance for me if I failed. As I readied myself for university, it seemed that all I could remember about Neuroanatomy was that I couldn't recall any of the multitude of details that define the complexities of the central nervous system—God's masterpiece of human "doing," "saying,"and "being."

Had I studied faithfully?—YES! in fact, the year had passed in a blur of classes, labs, and endless hours of study—rhythmically punctuated each week by twenty-four hours of blessed Sabbath worship and rest. Had I asked God to help me learn? YES!! I began and ended each day with prayer. I knew that I needed a solid foundation of basic sciences for the practice of competent medicine.

As despair enveloped me that morning, my eyes caught sight of a small box—a promise box containing hundreds of Bible promises, each one printed on a miniature scroll. The box was a gift from my grade-school teacher, given when I had been hospitalized a decade before. I selected one of the hundreds of mini scrolls and read the words of Jeremiah 31:16.

The promise was stunningly relevant to me that morning. The promise lingered with me as I joined the mass of bustling humanity streaming to their various responsibilities in the city. The promise calmed me as I entered the large exam room and took my seat along with the other 350 medical students in my class. The promise focused me as I responded to the essay questions with clarity and fresh recall.

Today, thirty-five years later, I treasure the First Place Certificate of the Gilbert G. Phillip Prize for neuroanatomy because it links me in a tangible way to the surety of God's promises.

This is what the Lord says: "Restrain your voice from weeping and your eyes from tears, for your work will be rewarded." Jeremiah 31:16, NIV

B. Lyn Behrens is president of Loma Linda University in Loma Linda, California. She graduated from Sydney University in 1964.

LESSON IN A CHOCOLATE KISS *By Gerald Kovalski*

One warm spring evening in Tennessee, the campus of Southern Missionary College murmured softly with the sounds of casual socializing, for which it is well known.

As the two of us strolled along the sidewalk, we came to a place where a tree cast a shadow from the streetlight. I reached for a kiss but got a piece of chocolate candy instead. The chocolate was good, but I sensed that something was wrong.

I had known Sandra most of the school year, and we had only recently started dating. At the women's dorm, where I had just picked her up, the dean said something that irritated the fellows. Out of earshot of the dean, I responded with some unflattering comments and apparently displayed a bit of temper. This did not set well with Sandra. She shared her feelings after the bite of chocolate.

From the first time I met her, I was attracted to Sandra and had worked hard to impress her. I realized at that moment that I was close to losing the ground I had gained in a relationship I now treasured. She wanted no part of someone who could not control his emotions or was willing to be hurtful to another person.

In the days and weeks that followed, our friendship grew. I kept my focus on controlling my quick and unflattering responses. There was no way I was going to lose this special friend or damage this developing relationship. I determined to rise to her standard.

It happens that way. We are willing to recognize our weaknesses and change to please someone we love! The same is true in our relationship with Christ. Because we love Him, we are not only willing, but anxious to please Him. His expectations are high, but because we want to continue our developing relationship, we rise to His standard.

Sandra and I have been married for more than thirty years. I'm still rising.

I led them with cords of human kindness, with ties of love; I lifted the yoke from their neck and bent down to feed them. Hosea 11:4, NIV

Gerald Kovalski is vice president for education of the Florida Conference of Seventh-day Adventists in Winter Park, Florida. He graduated from Southern College in 1963.

AN ANGEL STORY *By Don Jacobsen*

Whenever I hitchhiked, I always hoped for a late-model car. This time, I got one: an almost-new Plymouth convertible—and red. Even though the top was up, this was going to be an extraordinary trip. I was thumbing back to college from a weekend leave in the early 1950s, when hitchhiking was a lot safer.

The driver was clean-cut, forty-something, and we got acquainted as we drove along. He asked where I was going, and when I told him where the school was, he said he was headed near there and would be glad to drop me at the door. Outstanding. But it was about to get better.

We had driven about half an hour, and I had told him I was a ministerial student. On the edge of one of the little towns, he began to slow down and asked me if I wanted to drive. He had been up late the night before, he said, and would be grateful for a nap. I got behind the wheel, and he climbed into the back seat.

He had slept for about an hour when it dawned on me what was happening. Here I was, a struggling theology student, needing dependable transportation, and the man in the back seat was an angel. By and by, I would turn around, he would be gone, and the car would be mine!

Problem: What about the title and registration? Well, if God could provide the Plymouth and the angel driver, a simple thing like a government document wouldn't trouble Him. I smiled. It *did* pay to return a faithful tithe. What a stewardship story I would be able to tell.

I glanced often in the mirror, fully expecting to find the back seat empty.

As we got closer to campus, with the angel still in the car, I decided God was just testing my faith. But I never questioned what I knew He was about to do.

When I pulled up beside Sittner Hall and he sat up, I knew the story was not going to read as I had scripted it. I grabbed my suitcase, thanked him for the ride, and stood there watching as he drove away—in *my* car.

I have lived long enough to be thankful I didn't get the car. I generally grow better from struggle than from handouts. Eventually I got a set of wheels; eventually I got them paid for. God kept His promise—I had everything I needed. He still does—I still do.

My God shall supply all your need. Philippians 4:19

Don Jacobsen is assistant to the president of the North American Division of Seventh-day Adventists in Silver Spring, Maryland. He graduated from Walla Walla College in 1955.

FACULTY MADE
THE DIFFERENCE *By Peter D. H. Bath*

My wife and I joined the Adventist Church through baptism on November 17, 1977. Six weeks later, we entered the seminary at Andrews University. Behind all of that activity lies the wonderful leading of our Lord through His Word and through people who dedicated themselves to His service in education.

The seminary has been my only student experience with Adventist higher education. I found it formative, instructive, and directive in my life and the life of our family.

The journey began in August of 1977 with a quick visit to the seminary. At a Sabbath-afternoon potluck arranged by friends, we met Dr. Stephen Vitrano. At that time, my wife and I were in the throes of deciding what the Lord's will was for our lives. Cathy and I were still Anglicans, and Steve talked lovingly and affirmingly about the teachings of Anglicanism and the wonderful call that God provides to the people of all faiths. Cathy and I quickly learned that one of the significant advantages of Adventist higher education and, in particular, the seminary, was the quality of the individuals with whom we had the privilege of learning and working.

Harold Coffin was one of my first lecturers. He opened the portal of science and religion for us in a way that was truly inspiring. His quiet ways drew us to reflect upon the biblical and scientific evidence for Creation and the Flood. His personal touch invited us to a closer relationship with him and his family as we shared many a meal and visit together and saw the personal side of Adventism.

One of the most difficult aspects of embracing this new church and a new faith was knowing so few people. The seminary opened for us the opportunity to become acquainted with many remarkable people through those who took time to care and to show the way.

The seminary was exciting, stimulating, and very challenging. However, in the midst of this, we always had the opportunity to develop community and relationships with faculty and staff that proved to be very important in sustaining and guiding us. As we look back upon our years at Andrews, we consider them to be the "good ol' days," when life appeared to be a little simpler! I cherish the memory of our time there, and particularly the relationships that we forged with people like Steve Vitrano, Harold Coffin, Raoul Dederen, Walter Douglas, Des Cummings, and many others who made a world of difference in our lives.

Encourage one another and build each other up. 1 Thessalonians 5:11, NIV

Peter D. H. Bath is president of Kettering College of Medical Arts in Kettering, Ohio. He graduated from the University of Western Ontario in 1975.

COMPETING WITH CHEATERS *By David Freedman*

When I started college at a public university in 1975, I looked forward to beginning my studies in pre-med. I was thrilled by the great things a skilled surgeon could do to help others. I thought saving lives would be the greatest thing I could possibly do.

I learned an important lesson from an experience during a biology midterm exam during the second semester of my freshman year. Approximately eighty-five students met in a college amphitheater. After appropriate instructions from the professor, we began writing the exam. While I worked on mine, I watched four of the brightest students in our program sitting with a cheat sheet by their side. I was very upset, because I was trying to compete against these pre-med students who were now likely to receive some of the highest scores. The professor was oblivious to the cheating, but I was an eyewitness.

Fortunately, I soon was able to discuss this incident with my father.

He reminded me that we reap what we sow. Even though those cheaters might receive the highest grade on the test, what they had done was wrong. I was thankful that my upbringing prevented me from ever considering cheating.

Even though I faced fierce competition to excel and succeed in that premed program, I determined to put God's standards of honesty and integrity above everything else. I learned that if I put God first, He will direct my life. Furthermore, I needed to put forth the time and the effort in my studies in order to master the information I was expected to know. The Bible helped me to develop a healthy honesty and a work ethic grounded in integrity.

That experience helped me determine to do right simply because it is right. When I honor God in the small, everyday things, He will honor me. When I follow God in all His ways He will lead me into the path He wants me to follow.

Interestingly, God led me away from a career in the medical field and into the gospel ministry. So now I have the greatest opportunity for saving lives known to humanity: the proclamation of the gospel.

A faithful man will abound with blessings, but he who hastens to be rich will not go unpunished. Proverbs 28:20, RSV

David Freedman is secretary-treasurer of the Alaska Conference of Seventh-day Adventists in Anchorage, Alaska. He graduated from Rutgers University in 1979.

AT THE CROSSROADS *By Stan B. Berry*

My first day as a freshman at Pacific Union College was filled with orientation sessions and athletic tests—the latter conducted in the heat of the afternoon sun. That evening I lay on the bottom tier of a metal bunk in Newton Hall contemplating my situation between bouts of nausea. It almost seemed to me I might have been abducted by aliens. Everything was strange—the surroundings, the food, even the smells.

My journey between two very different "worlds" had been brief and tumultuous. In the spring of 1971, I graduated with honors from an all-male Catholic high school in Napa, California. I was a four-sport lettered athlete, a nominal Christian, and a full participant in the mainstream culture of the day. Two prestigious universities had sent me letters of acceptance, and a state scholarship from Governor Ronald Reagan would cover the bulk of my tuition costs. I planned to spend a carefree summer working. My only worry was being drafted. Then my parents dropped a bombshell on my well-laid plans.

Mom and Dad had become Adventists during the previous year. Over time, their spiritual conversion was augmented by a cultural conversion. I had become accustomed to green casseroles, midweek Bible studies, and weekend TV droughts. I even attended church on occasion. But the thought of joining what I thought to be a very odd denomination that abstained from dancing and drinking and went to church on Saturdays was out of the question. You can imagine my shock when they requested that I attend the nearby Seventh-day Adventist college—"Cracker-Hill"—the derisive name given to the Howell Mountain college by my Catholic schoolmates.

I still remember the heated arguments that followed. Growing up, I had rarely gone against my parents' wishes, but this was asking too much.

Three events that summer finally persuaded me to give PUC a chance. After a particularly rancorous debate with my parents, I announced that I was moving out for good. My rebellious determination was no match for my father's tears. I had never seen this bear of a man cry before, and I was deeply moved. Then Brother Richard, vice-principal of my Catholic high school and a friend, counseled me to follow my parents' wishes. (Think of that: a Catholic cleric encouraging a young person to attend a Protestant college, an Adventist one at that). Finally, I spent a week backpacking in the High Sierras with three PUC students, one of whom was from my hometown of Sonoma. I found them to be pretty regular guys except that they were vegetarians and didn't use coarse language.

So that fall I enrolled at PUC. The first few days were the toughest because I had to make many adjustments, and my classmates had to make some adjustments for me. But along the way, many people—roommates, other students, professors, staff members, and even people within the community—made me feel at home. Eventually I was baptized, married a wonderful Adventist girl, and went to work for Adventist Health System/West. I am ever so thankful for the special people God sent to influence my life at a time when my chosen path could have easily lead me away from the Seventh-day Adventist Church, away from a Christian lifestyle, or from a lifelong relationship with Christ.

Trust in the Lord with all your heart and lean not on your own understanding; in all your ways acknowledge him, and he will direct your paths. Proverbs 3:5, 6, margin, NIV

Stan B. Berry is president and chief executive officer of Hanford Community Medical Center in Hanford, California. He graduated from Loma Linda University in 1976.

THE LONG WAY HOME *By G. Alexander Bryant*

As many college students do during finals, I had just gone two days without sleep. Now, after the tests, I was looking forward to going home for the six-week Thanksgiving–Christmas break. But a complication arose. My car had mechanical problems. I had planned to follow my friend Elaine home in my car. She was going to show me a shortcut to St. Louis. My car problems were holding us up.

Elaine asked me to leave my car and ride with her and some friends back to St. Louis. I said I really wanted to drive my car back and hoped she'd wait. I feverishly began working to take my water pump off. It was cold, misty, and damp. Every time I tried to unloosen the bolt, my hand would hit the side of the car or a metal part, and it was very painful. Soon I was angry and upset with the Lord, wondering why He was taking me through this. Several hours passed while I ran back and forth to the auto supply store, trying to get all the parts required for the repair. Finally I gave up and told Elaine to go on ahead. I'd go the old way, which would take three hours longer.

About an hour after they left, my car repair work suddenly came together quickly and smoothly. Soon I was on the road, driving the old route home. By then, it was late in the evening, and it wasn't long before I got tired and sleepy. I stopped in Memphis to call home to get an uncle's address, where I wanted to spend the night. When the phone at home was answered, I was greeted by a hysterical voice on the other end. It was my father, and he was frantic, asking where I was and if I was all right.

When he calmed down, he told me that Elaine, had been killed in an accident, and several others in her car had been injured. Tears ran down my face. My friend was gone. And I recalled how upset I was with God just a few hours earlier because of the condition of my car. Now I realized that God, in His wisdom, had been looking out for me the whole time.

There is a way which seems right to a man, but its end is the way of death. Proverbs 14:12, NKJV

G. Alexander Bryant is youth ministries director and education superintendent of the Central States Conference of Seventh-day Adventists in Kansas City, Kansas. He graduated from Oakwood College in 1981.

E-MAIL: 1967 *By Newton Hoilette*

Registration for the new term at West Indies College was rapidly approaching, and I was out of money. I didn't even have enough money to go home to get money. I prayed all week long. I asked Aussie for money; I asked Franco; I asked T.G. None of them had money. It was a bad time for everyone. I needed just five shillings (in 1967, that was approximately forty-five cents U.S.) to travel by bus to my home. There I could arrange for the money I needed for registration.

Friday came, and I had classes until noon. Yet I was convinced, through faith, that I was going to receive the money I needed to make the trip home for the weekend. "I don't know how, but I know I'm going," I remarked to a friend as we walked out of the classroom. I really expected to go that day!

As I walked by the administration building, Vivia called out from the post office window, "Newton, there's mail here for you." I rushed to the window and received my expected mail. I tore open the letter and found it was from my brother Brandon in New York City. This was highly unusual. We never wrote to each other. Yet somehow he had been impressed to write just in time for that letter to arrive shortly after noon that Friday when I needed so desperately to go home.

Enclosed in his letter was one dollar, just *one dollar!!* The exchange rate for one American dollar was seven shillings and sixpence in the British currency in Jamaica. What relief, what joy came to my heart as I considered how God had prepared the answer to my prayer. That mail was the most exciting thing that had ever happened to me in college.

Through God's providence, that one dollar provided my fare from the college to my home, with enough left to return tithe. The answer to my need came through faith and prayer. In 1967, it took five days for mail to travel from New York to Jamaica. Before I called on God, He was already answering my prayer; Brandon had already mailed the letter!

That memorable Friday, while I was yet speaking, God heard my call. The sequence of events gave the appearance that the mail had arrived instantly upon my request. Like electronic communication today, it created an immediate answer to my need! Looking back now to 1967, I see it as my first encounter with "e-mail!"

Before they call, I will answer; and while they are yet speaking, I will hear. Isaiah 65:24

Newton Hoilette is vice president for student affairs of Andrews University in Berrien Springs, Michigan. He graduated from West Indies College in 1968.

GOD'S GENTLE LEADING *By Reo E. Ganson*

Canadian Union College certainly had seen many young men and women with more mischievous energy than I had. But I had my share.

My parents raised my brothers and me on a small farm. When we were in high school, they sold the small farm and moved the family close to Canadian Union College. This allowed us to walk to classes, and yet we still had the advantage of living at home.

Although my parents were well meaning in this decision, it had a downside. We had an abundance of spare time. During the first years of college, study hadn't yet become a priority for me. My behavior often turned to mischief instead of activities constructive to the college or to myself. After one particular escapade, the administration decided that the time had come for a little well-designed discipline. They felt it might provide my parents some assistance in achieving their worthy goals for their son.

They sent me over to the college farm for a stint of free labor.

The morning was still dark when I climbed into the farm manager's truck. We had to haul home several tons of feed from a supplier several hours' drive from the college.

Although the long drive was uneventful as far as the work was concerned, it did provide many hours for quiet, meaningful discussion. There in the cab of that truck, a major part of the direction of my life was determined—not in an obvious, surface way, but hidden down deep in my will. During that long ride, the farm manager, in his own humble way, invited me to a life of service to our Lord as a gospel minister.

Today, I've worked for nearly thirty years in the education system of the Seventh-day Adventist Church, as an elementary-school teacher, principal, college teacher, and president. And through it all, I have considered myself a gospel minister in the best sense of what that farm manager meant. And even now, I also serve as a volunteer pastor for a small Adventist church. The quiet but firm decision I made in that old farm truck on the encouragement of a dedicated staff member has been a guiding principle in my life ever since.

He shall feed his flock like a shepherd: he shall gather the lambs with his arm, and carry them in his bosom, and shall gently lead those that are with young. Isaiah 40:11

Reo E. Ganson is associate director of education of the General Conference of Seventh-day Adventists in Silver Spring, Maryland. He graduated from Canadian Union College in 1963.

A CHALLENGING
SABBATH MORNING *By Darold Retzer*

One Sabbath, early in my sophomore year at La Sierra College, I woke early, with the sun streaming through the window of my room. The night before, discovering that I had no Sabbath-morning responsibilities, I had planned to sleep late and get up just in time for Sabbath School. But since I was wide awake, I decided to read my Bible.

Opening to 1 Timothy, I read Paul's counsel to a young preacher. It seemed pertinent because, as a theology major, I planned to be a preacher soon, and I was young. As I read, a verse jumped out at me. It seemed that God was speaking directly to me.

"Let no one despise your youth."

Wow, I thought, *I don't need to feel limited or inadequate because I am young.* I thought of Daniel and his companions, who were young, probably teenagers, when they were taken captive to Babylon. They stood true to God and for what they believed.

It was teenagers and young adults in the 1840s who took the leading role in what became the Seventh-day Adventist Church. Ellen White was only seventeen when she had her first vision and began sharing the good news with others. Annie R. Smith, a poet, died when she was only twenty-seven, having still made a significant editorial contribution to the advent movement in those few years. (Ten of her poems are hymns in the old *Church Hymnal,* and three are in the new.) Her brother, Uriah Smith, became editor of the *Review and Herald* at age 23.

From that bright, early-Sabbath morning, Paul's challenge to young Timothy to "be an example to the believers" became a personal challenge to me. More than just saying, "Don't let anyone look down on you because of your age," Paul challenges young adults to lead the way in holy living. "Be an example."

People around us may be living inconsistent lives. Even though we are young, we can set the pace for what the Lord would have His people be: people of faith *and* action, at any age.

Let no one despise your youth, but be an example to the believers in word, in conduct, in love, in spirit, in faith, in purity. 1 Timothy 4:12, NKJV

Darold Retzer is president of the Northern California Conference of Seventh-day Adventists in Pleasant Hill, California. He graduated from La Sierra University in 1964.

BUTTERMILK BREAKFASTS *By Bill Knott*

It was the buttermilk on the cornflakes that finally drove me to despair. I shoved my tray of uneaten food into the return rack, hurried back to my dorm room, and sobbed and sobbed.

I was probably the least-prepared victim of homesickness who ever went away to an Adventist college. Halfway through my college career, I arrived at Newbold College in the fall of 1977, convinced that the next few months were sure to be the most exhilarating of my nineteen years. As a confirmed Anglophile, I had devoured histories of England since I was a child and was halfway through a major in English literature just then. The chance to walk where Shakespeare had walked, where Elizabeth ruled, where generations of my ancestors had lived and died, filled me with a kind of holy wonderment. I settled into my first week of classes with a zest made up of one part adrenaline and two parts glee.

But then it started happening. Inexplicably (and embarrassingly), every morning as I ate breakfast in the cafeteria, a lump the size of a tennis ball would rise in my throat, my eyes would begin to brim with tears, and the food would stay uneaten on my tray. Newbold breakfasts being what they were in the late seventies, guys my size tried to eat everything allowable on the one pass through line in order to make it to lunch without fainting. Leaving any food on the plate was not a nutritional option.

Try as I might, the toast and juice and strange-tasting Weetabix simply wouldn't go down. It was the morning that I accidentally poured buttermilk instead of whole milk on my one and only bowl of cornflakes that broke this camel's back. Cornflakes and I have never liked each other; I detest buttermilk.

I sat on my bed that gray morning, sobbing from some deep center I didn't know I had, while the rational part of me tried to figure out what was happening. No, I wasn't classically homesick: I had certainly been away from Mom and Dad before for weeks at a time. And my stateside girlfriend and I weren't engaged in anything more serious than a terribly romantic transatlantic correspondence. Breakfast couldn't be the reason, either: at our house, breakfast was a fend-for-yourself kind of meal where you gulped your Wheaties before dashing out the door to school. It certainly hadn't been some warm, supportive time of family bonding like supper usually was.

So why the tears at breakfast? Between long, shivering sobs, I began asking God about it. I prayed from that newly discovered place inside me where all these powerful emotions had apparently been building up for days, asking for calmness and peace and the chance to get through journalism class without red eyes. And the answer came back that it was loneliness more than "homesickness" I was experiencing. It was that I was missing the sharing of my life with someone, anyone, who would listen for a moment, make eye contact, and be there again tomorrow.

"Find people; reach out to people; invest in people," God whispered to me that morning, "and wherever you are, you'll find a place you can call home."

In journalism class, I slipped a note to the American girl in the next row—and she smiled and wrote back. In Medieval English Lit, I made a crack about all things English that almost brought the British students out of their chairs, howling with wounded national pride and guaranteeing that someone would say something to me before the day was over!

By noon, I was sitting in the cafeteria, still alone, still wondering whether Marmite was an edible substance or a petroleum byproduct. But I also knew that God had given me a strategy that would help me survive in a place I so much wanted to be.

Cast all your anxiety on him because he cares for you. 1 Peter 5:7, NIV

Bill Knott is senior pastor of Walla Walla College Church in College Place, Washington. He graduated from Atlantic Union College in 1979.

A THANKSGIVING
TO REMEMBER   *By Ramona Perez Greek*

After my father's death, and a year or so after I had graduated from academy, I started thinking seriously about my life. I wanted a different life than the hard struggle my mother and father experienced so often as migrant workers. I decided to go to college and receive a formal education. This seemed an impossible goal when basic survival, and not education, was the priority in our lives as migrants.

Since Hispanic families are very close-knit, I was highly reluctant to ask my mother if I could leave home to attend college. When I finally did ask, she said she needed me at home to help her raise the seven other small children in our family. Now that my mother was alone, I knew that the burden of raising the children was particularly heavy. And yet my heart was set on going to college too.

After a brief time of disappointment and much prayer, I asked Mother about working out a plan that would allow me to meet my dream of attending college. I said, "Yes, Mother, I can help you, but you must let me move the family to the college so that I can attend, and help you with the children at the same time." I had chosen Pacific Union College in California, which was approximately eight hours away from our home by car.

Through God's grace, my mother accepted the challenge to move. Since school was to start soon, she stipulated that I would have to take the children ahead on my own while she stayed back to close out responsibilities where we lived.

I was thrilled to be at college, at last! However, my first day on the campus caused me great anxiety. I was just as anxious as I had been the night before, when I drove up that unfamiliar, narrow, winding road to the college through pea-soup fog. I was a stranger to a college environment, and with other cultural and language barriers, I felt unsettled and unsure: Where to go? Where to start? How to find housing? How and where to find jobs? How to enroll in college? How to enroll my brothers and sisters in the elementary school and academy? Learning and then managing all these complicated steps in the educational process was trying for an inexperienced young girl like me.

Through faith and trust, God opened doors that seemed impossible, and within a few days we had found a house, the children were enrolled in school, and I started my college classes.

The weeks moved quickly, and Thanksgiving approached. Mother wrote to let us know she was finally able to move. She would arrive Thanksgiving Day.

The night before Thanksgiving, we had no food and no money to purchase any, because I had paid all the money we had toward tuition. The youngest child was four years of age. How would he and the other little ones understand that there would be no food on Thanksgiving Day?

As the oldest one at home and in the absence of my mother, I did what I had watched her do often. I asked the little ones to kneel down in prayer. We would take our troubles to God, and somehow I knew He would answer.

As soon as we had completed our prayer and the last "amen" was said, there was a knock on the door.

I brushed my knees as I arose, wondering who it could be at this hour of the night. I opened the door, and there stood several Pathfinders dressed in their uniforms, holding boxes filled with food. They walked into the house and placed the boxes down in the empty living room. They smiled and said, "Happy Thanksgiving!" and then they were gone as quickly as they had come. I have no idea how they knew our needs that day. I don't know if one of my little brothers or sisters shared our need at school, but I do know that God is a God of love and that His wisdom, grace, and love never fail us!

This story is meaningful to me, because it is my story, and I have learned that whatever my struggles, however large they loom, God promises to be with me. I have found Him to be true to His word! He is a constant and true Friend.

I am with you alway. Matthew 28:20

Ramona Perez Greek is assistant director of the office of women's ministries of the North American Division of Seventh-day Adventists and lives in Montgomery, Alabama. She graduated from Pacific Union College in 1972.

THE DIFFERENCE THAT PRAISE MAKES *By Charles Scriven*

When I edited my college newspaper, the back page of the year's last issue displayed a photograph of a cloud, backlit with sunshine, soaring past the silhouetted steeple of the campus church. Of the seniors about to graduate, the caption said, ". . . and they'll remember worship in the church."

I do remember. I remember Evensong late Sabbath afternoons. I remember grand festivals on Sabbath mornings, when the choir sang and the sanctuary shook with sound. I remember Friday nights, singing parts and hearing student missionaries tell their stories of adventure.

And more than I would have thought back then, it made me who I am.

Who I am, mind you, is no great shakes. I'm a struggler, amazed and sometimes alarmed by life's surprises. But I carry on the struggle in an atmosphere of hope. I carry on the struggle out of passionate regard for others. I carry on the struggle in full confidence that I can fall short and be forgiven.

It might have turned out differently. At my (middle) age, I could have slouched already into discouragement and shame. I could have diminished into a mere shadow of myself, with little to offer but a callous heart and a bad disposition.

But when, at church on my Christian campus, I sang songs to the honor of God and heard stories of my Maker's marvelous deeds, I became a self I could not otherwise have been. I became someone who saw a God-shaped world to enjoy and God-shaped life to lead and was lifted up from self-preoccupation to a higher plane of gratitude and generosity.

I remain a struggler, like every human being. But the worship I remember—the praise I offered in the fellowship of other Christians—made a difference that seems priceless now.

College is the ideal place to learn such life-enhancing song in a worshiping community. Praising God together in a community of inquisitive faith boosts our chances of carrying on life's struggle with dignity and hope—and an unbending decency in our relationships with others.

Isn't that what we want? And don't we want it more than anything else in the world?

O sing to the Lord a new song. . . . For great is the Lord, and greatly to be praised. Psalm 96:1, 4, RSV

Charles Scriven is president of Columbia Union College in Takoma Park, Maryland. He graduated from Walla Walla College in 1966.

A LABOR DAY MIRACLE *By A. David Jimenez*

On Labor Day weekend, 1973, at the beginning of my junior year in college, I decided to head home to Orlando, Florida. I loaded up my 1970 Opel station wagon with four of my best friends and hit the road. I didn't have a lot of money in college, and the little money I earned went toward tuition and other college expenses. So it wasn't surprising that the tires on my Opel were worn. We had enough money for gas, and that was all that really mattered. We turned south on Interstate 75 and began our journey.

As we crossed the Georgia/Florida border into Hamilton County, we got caught in one of the worst thunderstorms I had ever seen. That should have slowed me down, but I was in such a hurry I continued at the same speed. Passing the car in front of me, I hit a puddle that I didn't see. The car began to hydroplane. Heavily loaded as we were, the back end swerved toward the median, and we were going backward. Just as we hit the median, the car swerved again, and we were headed uncontrollably toward two oncoming trailer trucks. Before I could think, I jerked the steering wheel to avoid what seemed to be a sure collision . . . and a miracle occurred. Those badly worn tires instantly grabbed the pavement and jerked us back into the median. The trucks flew past, missing us by inches.

For several moments, we were all silent. No one knew what to say. When we inspected the car, the only damage we found was a flat tire. We stood in amazement at what we knew could only have been the hand of God at work. Gathering in a circle, we whispered a word of prayer, each of us acknowledging the miracle that had occurred.

He shall give his angels charge over thee, to keep thee in all thy ways. Psalm 91:11

A. David Jimenez is president and cheif executive officer of Huguley Memorial Medical Center in Fort Worth, Texas. He graduated from Southern College in 1975.

ELECTION LESSON *By LuAnn Wolfe Davis*

The Business Club nominating committee was to find candidates willing to hold the various club offices for the next school year. After we had nominated two male candidates for club president, one committee member suggested it was the eighties and perhaps a woman should be included on the ballot for president.

The Business Club faculty advisor looked my way and asked if I would like to be that woman. At first, I was upset by the suggestion that I be the token female on the ballot, included only for the sake of appearances.

But I decided to accept the nomination. Then and there, I also vowed I would win the election. On the day of the election, the candidates gave speeches. I was nervous, yet confident. By now, I was adamant that there was no reason a woman couldn't be president of the Business Club.

After we made our speeches, we waited in the hallway while a hand vote was tallied. It seemed to take an extraordinarily long time to count the vote. I learned later that several votes had to be taken because of ties. But when the final count was taken, I had won! I had accepted the challenge. Now I had to live up to it.

The next school year, the Business Club sponsored an educational or social activity every month. We added new club programs. The club had never been so active. Of course, I wasn't solely responsible for these successes, because I benefited from a fantastic group of fellow officers, and we worked together like a real team.

Even though it all started with my assumption that I was just a token, good things came from it. I learned a valuable spiritual lesson. The Bible describes a worthy woman in Proverbs 31. Verses 25 and 26 state, "Strength and dignity are her clothing, and she smiles at the future. She opens her mouth in wisdom, and the teaching of kindness is on her tongue" (NASB). As a woman, I can either accept tokenism and limit myself to certain possibilities in life; or I can challenge the future by using my strength, dignity, wisdom, and faith in the Lord to accomplish anything.

There's a wonderful world out there; and regardless of our gender, we must not let anyone hinder us from accomplishing what the Lord wants for us out of life!

Then you shall prosper, if you are careful to observe the statutes and the ordinances which the Lord commanded. . . . Be strong and courageous, do not fear nor be dismayed. 1 Chronicles 22:13, NASB

LuAnn Wolfe Davis is vice president for advancement of Union College in Lincoln, Nebraska. She graduated from the same institution in 1982.

ME AND THE 144,000 *By Edward Motschiedler*

During my sophomore year at Andrews University, I lost hope and discovered the gospel. This did not happen at the same time, of course, but in the same year. I lost hope when I heard my Bible teacher say that only a few people would be saved. I discovered the gospel when the Week of Prayer speaker said that anyone could be saved.

My Bible teacher emphasized that only 144,000 would go through the time of trouble and be ready for Jesus to come. At that time, there were about three million Seventh-day Adventists. One night, after the lights had been turned out in old Birch Hall, my roommate and I discussed the odds of being among the saved. If only 144,000 of three million people were going to be saved, that meant that we would have to beat out 2,856,000 people to make it into heaven. As we discussed our spiritual life, we both reached a scary conclusion. We were probably not even in the top million, to say nothing of the top 144,000. We both concluded that if we were not going to make it, why even try. This led me to a detour over "fools hill."

I am not proud of many of the things I did that year.

During the spring Week of Prayer, I took my body to the required meetings but not my soul. However, early in the week, Elder E. L. Minchin told us it was God's will that all be saved (see 2 Peter 3:9). I decided to challenge Elder Minchin about the differences between his teaching and my Bible teacher's. He told me that Revelation 7:4 did talk about a group of 144,000, but Revelation 7:9 mentions a group in heaven so great that none could number them. He then led me to accept Christ's atonement and to believe in His power to save even me.

The good news of the gospel is that Christ has already paid the penalty for our sins. His gift, not our works, entitles us to heaven.

That Friday night, I went to the front of Pioneer Memorial Church and stood in the pulpit to testify of my new assurance of salvation. After my testimony, Elder Minchin said to me, "May God send you on to be a great witness for Him." That has been my determination and vocation ever since.

The Lord is not slow in keeping his promise, as some understand slowness. He is patient with you, not wanting anyone to perish, but everyone to come to repentance. 2 Peter 3:9, NIV

Edward Motschiedler is president of the Ohio Conference of Seventh-day Adventists in Mt. Vernon, Ohio. He graduated from Southern College in 1963.

A QUIET PLACE *By Delbert W. Baker*

The park behind the playing field at Oakwood College was a quiet place for me during my college years. It wasn't large or elaborate or extraordinary. It was just a park. Yet the attraction was there—the stately trees, the earthy smell of nature, the grandeur of the sky that peeked through the tops of the trees, and the quiet stillness. All this added to the appeal that made the place special.

The park was a place to get away, a place to do some reflection, praying, thinking. It offered privacy, solitude, and escape from the stress of study and the busyness of college life. It was here that I learned the power of place and the calming influence of meditation. As a result, I came to better appreciate the words of the psalmist when he wrote: "Oh that I had wings like a dove! for then would I fly away, and be at rest" (Psalm 55:6).

The park played a role in the major decisions I made during my college years. The decisions to accept Christ as personal Saviour, marry my college sweetheart, and accept a call to the ministry were all made or molded in that park. My appreciation for a quiet place wasn't philosophical or intellectual. I simply needed the time and place to reflect and think. The park offered me that opportunity.

What did I do in the park? I don't recall ever really having a list of things to do. I was involved in student government, prison ministry, literature evangelism, the ministerial extern program, and of course, studies. But the park offered a break from all that. Sometimes I would go there and think, mediate, dream, work through issues. Other times I would invite a friend or even a small group. Most of the time, however, I wanted to be alone.

One of the habits I developed in connection with my quiet place is what I called "prepraying." I would ask God to prepare me "now" for what was to come in the future. Prepraying helped me to trust in God's providence. I think this habit was one of the most helpful ones that I nurtured during my college years. God has answered and even now is answering many of the items for which I claimed God's blessings in advance during those times.

All of us have different needs, but it seems to be fairly clear that the human spirit needs time to revive and a place to heal. The years have passed and circumstances have changed, yet I still need a quiet place.

Woe unto them that join house to house, that lay field to field, till there be no place, that they may be placed alone in the midst of the earth! Isaiah 5:8.

Delbert W. Baker is special assistant to the president and director of diversity of Loma Linda University in Loma Linda, California. He graduated from Oakwood College in 1975.

HE LOOSED MY TONGUE *By Herman Bauman*

I had assumed God was perfect; that He never made a mistake. However, when He called me as a young teenager to be a preacher, I knew He had made a huge mistake.

I was petrified in front of an audience. One time, my home church—of six members—asked me to read the mission story. I stood up, read two sentences, and said, "I can't do it," and sat down. When I was a student at Hylandale Academy, I was invited to speak at a nursing home. On the way back to the academy after the services, all the kids laughed at me because I had done such a horrible job. I did not have the talent to be a preacher, yet *God* had called me.

The principal of the academy said, "Herman, I don't believe God called you to be a preacher. You know, you could be a farmer and still be a witness for Him." My girlfriend painfully explained to me, "I know you love the Lord and really want to serve Him, but I just don't believe you have what it takes to be a preacher."

In spite of the counsel and my own recognition of my hopelessness, I enrolled in Southern Missionary College as a theology student. I knew I couldn't do it, but *God* had called me.

I took courage from Moses' experience in the wilderness. When God called him to go back to Egypt to lead His people out of bondage, he said: "I am not eloquent . . . I am slow of speech and of tongue." Wow! That sounded just like me. But what assurance God gave him! "Now therefore go, and I will be with your mouth" (Exodus 4:10, 12, RSV). If God could do it for Moses, couldn't He do it for me?

One thing especially encouraged me. Jesus was coming very soon, surely before I ever graduated from college. Then I would never have to worry about going out into the ministry. Still I had to prepare, so I took advantage of every opportunity to gain confidence and get experience. I asked to join the American Temperance Society team that would go all over the Southern Union to put on programs. Adrian Lauritzen, the sponsor, let me be one of the speakers. I made careful preparation of my short speech and prayed for God's help. I will never forget our first presentation. It was at the college, among friends. Shaking from head to toe, I got up and gave my speech. It was horrible. People laughed at me. I kept trying, struggling, and failing miserably, but God continued to say, "I've called you to be a preacher."

And then one day it happened. We were in Meridian, Mississippi. Oh, what a vivid memory I have of it. Our team presented its usual program, but when I got up to speak, things were *not* usual. God performed a miracle. He "loosed my tongue." He gave me freedom to speak. He gave me confidence, and I presented my talk with an enthusiasm, effectiveness, and power that surprised me and shocked my fellow team members. After the program, they asked, "What happened to you?" My only response was, "God performed a miracle." And God has been performing that miracle ever since. I am so grateful that God chose to "be with my mouth" as He was with Moses and that "all His biddings are enablings."

Ray Boltz, popular contemporary gospel singer, has a song that never fails to touch me deeply. It's entitled "Here Comes a Miracle." The next time you see me, you can point to me and shout that phrase, "Here comes a miracle," and it will be absolutely true. Oh, how I thank and praise God!

"As the will of man co-operates with the will of God, it becomes omnipotent. Whatever is to be done at His command may be accomplished in His strength. All His biddings are enablings" (*Christ Object Lessons*, 333).

Who has made man's mouth? . . . Is it not I, the Lord? Now therefore go, and I will be with your mouth and teach you what you shall speak. Exodus 4:11, 12, RSV

Herman Bauman is president of the Arizona Conference of Seventh-day Adventists in Scottsdale, Arizona. He graduated from Andrews University in 1958.

SOMEONE IS
WATCHING ME *By Nathaniel G. Higgs*

It was my responsibility to keep the basement tidy in Green Hall, the library building. Each evening, I cleaned the restrooms and buffed the tile floor. I was busy as usual one evening when I was interrupted by the familiar voice of a campus coed, who, with her book in hand, asked me to assist her with English. Since I was attracted to Christine, and English was my specialty, I graciously agreed. Cutting off the buffer, I started toward the stairs that would take us to the library reading room, where I would assist her with diagraming.

Just as I stepped on the first step, the sleeve of my jacket, which was turned up, caught the light switch, and we suddenly found ourselves in complete darkness. Instinctively, I flicked on the light switch, and there was light again. Yet in that second of time, the dean of the college began to descend the stairs. He was one who would not believe the truth even if it struck him with the force of lightning. What should I do? In that moment of panic, I ran, only to be discovered by the old sage.

I had done no wrong! Yet from all appearances I was as guilty as sin. All my explanations were to no avail. I had borne a false witness. My actions had spoken louder than my words. His perception became, in effect, reality.

What impressions do I give to those who observe me? The apostle Paul teaches us to avoid the appearance of evil. This does not prohibit me from doing right simply because it may appear wrong to some onlooker. But in the work of righteousness, I must beware of evil. If the propriety of an action is doubtful or bordering on the edge of evil, then my duty is to avoid it. I must live an open life, free from the shadowy insinuations of wrong.

On campus, there are many social choices to make: friends, entertainment, leisure time, habits of speech, etc. Avoid compromising places of amusement and friends that will mark you as "that kind." If I am honest in my thoughts, my actions will reflect it. Righteousness never compromises on the periphery of impropriety. Someone is watching me, whom I will influence for right or for wrong.

Abstain from all appearance of evil. 1 Thessalonians 5:22.

Nathaniel G. Higgs is superintendent of schools of the South Central Conference of Seventh-day Adventists in Nashville, Tennessee. He graduated from Oakwood College in 1965.

THE HUMAN FACE OF GOD'S LOVE *By J. Bjornar Storfjell*

People who did the decent thing of being genuinely friendly and concerned stand out far above anything else when I reflect on my college years. I had come as a young foreign student with a strange, unpronounceable name to Walla Walla College in the early 1960s. Far from home and with no financial support, I worked the best I could while studying in a foreign language and in an even more foreign educational system.

The faculty members in the theology department, without fail, willingly took time to explain both the curriculum and subjects that came up in the classes. Richard Litke could even throw a Norwegian word into the conversation now and then. These teachers helped me to keep my goals in focus. They opened up for me the biblical world and helped me to experience its reality, even to make its study my career.

But as the riches of the past increased, the riches of the present were soon spent on tuition, room and board, and various other needs. Before too long, the business manager informed me of that which I already knew: my money was all gone, and a sizable bill still had to be paid. With no immediate resources available, I was told I had to leave school.

The academic dean, Hans Rasmussen, who in his soft Danish accent was even able to pronounce my name correctly, happened into the business manager's office while the unpleasant reality of my situation was spelled out. In a genuinely warm and caring way, he insisted that I should remain in school, and then he helped work out a plan to make it possible.

I have often thought about the impact Litke and Rasmussen had on my life. In an already-Christian institution, they became both the voice and the hand of God for me by bringing my studies into sharper focus and making it possible for me to stay in school. In the care of such teachers and administrators, I learned that the love of God is most effective when it has a human face.

The King will answer and say to them, "Truly I say to you, to the extent that you did it to one of these brothers of Mine, even the least of them, you did it to Me. Matthew 25:40, NASB

J. Bjornar Storfjell is professor of archaeology and history of antiquity at the Seventh-day Adventist Theological Seminary at Andrews University in Berrien Springs, Michigan. He graduated from Walla Walla College in 1966.

GO IN! *By Thomas J. Mostert, Jr.*

By the end of my freshman year, I was not entirely comfortable with my major in theology. True, some events in the previous months seemed to indicate that the ministry was God's plan for my life. But so many doubts remained that I was seriously thinking of making a change.

If only I could really know what God wanted. How I wished for a sign from Him. Yet I knew that signs could be counterfeited or misunderstood, and thus were not always safe. So I didn't ask for a sign. I simply prayed earnestly for some clear indication to erase my doubts.

What happened next has influenced my life in a profound way to this very day. My roommate and a number of other students had been recruited for literature evangelism work during the summer. They were holding their final campus meeting in the chapel before starting their summer's work. I wasn't among them. I had another job already lined up where I would earn all I needed for the next year's expenses. Not for a moment had I considered risking my college career on the uncertainty of a sales job as a student literature evangelist.

That day, I walked past the chapel where the recruits were meeting, thankful not to be among them. Suddenly, out of nowhere came a commanding voice: "GO IN!" Just two words. I looked all around me, surprised at this tactic—bold even for LE recruiters. No one was there. I started down the stairs to leave the building, when the voice came a second time: "GO IN!" By now I was agitated, but I confirmed that *there was no one around*.

Again I started to move away, only to hear those same two words spoken with such authority a third time that I turned and walked into the chapel in a daze.

That summer of bookselling was a success and filled with miracles. It sealed forever any doubts I had about God's will for my life. Never since has He chosen to communicate with me in a literal voice. But I will never forget that life-changing encounter in answer to my sincere request for guidance. Thirty-five years later, I can still hear those words as though they came today.

Listen to my cry for help, my King and my God, for to you I pray. In the morning, O Lord, you hear my voice; in the morning I lay my requests before you and wait in expectation. Psalm 5:2, 3, NIV

Thomas J. Mostert, Jr., is president of the Pacific Union Conference of Seventh-day Adventists in Westlake Village, California, and chairman of the board of Pacific Union College. He graduated from Southern College in 1963.

YOU'RE AN ANGEL By Esther Ramharacksingh Knott

It was spring break. I decided to join a school-sponsored backpack trip to the foothills of the Great Smoky Mountains. I found a friend willing to lend me his equipment. He was more than six feet tall, and his backpack clearly wasn't designed for my five-foot-three frame. I knew I was in trouble when first I filled the backpack, put it on, and fell over backward. I clambered on the bus anyway.

As we began our trek, three of the eight in our group went on ahead of me. Two couples lagged behind. Soon it was dusk, and I found myself all alone on the mountain with my pack getting very heavy. I shifted the weight from one shoulder to the other and then from my shoulders to my hips. Nothing seemed to help. I took the pack off and tried carrying it in front of me, but that didn't work either. How could I get myself, my own supplies, and my share of the group supplies to the campsite? I thought of leaving a trail of supplies that those behind could pick up. Perhaps a bear would come out of the woods and relieve me of my burden. Then the group couldn't blame me for not pulling my share of the load.

In my desperation, I knelt and prayed. "Dear God, please send an angel to carry my pack. In the Uncle Arthur *Bedtime Stories*, You always sent help [I actually said that]. I need help. Send an angel, disguised as a man, to come over the mountain and help me. I *know* You can do this if You choose. Amen."

As I got off my knees, I heard someone whistling. God was quick! It was one of our group members. "There you are!" he said. "We hadn't seen you in a while, so I decided to run ahead to try and find you. The group's about half a mile behind." He looked at me a little bewildered when I started exclaiming, "You're an angel! You're an angel!" Then out tumbled the story of my despair and my prayer. He took my pack, balanced it on his head, his pack, and his guitar. Together, we went running down the mountain, singing!

So, did God send an angel? My answer is an emphatic "Yes!" I read a quote a few years ago that went something like this: "We are each of us angels with only one wing, and we only fly by embracing one another." I'm committed to flying. That means I must embrace others and help others bear their "burdens." May God use me today to answer a prayer, to help someone else fly.

Bear one another's burdens, and so fulfil the law of Christ. Galatians 6:2, RSV

Esther Ramharacksingh Knott is associate pastor of Sligo Seventh-day Adventist Church in Takoma Park, Maryland. She graduated from Andrews University in 1980.

ON BEING A TEACHER – AND MY OWN SELF *By Paul Gordon*

My father was an ordained pastor in Washington. Preachers' kids often have a different experience than many others. Sometimes more is expected of them. And sometimes, some of them rebel against those expectations.

When I entered college in 1948, I tried to keep my family background to myself. I wanted to be known and accepted for my own self, and not as somebody else's son.

Unfortunately, one of my college teachers knew my father. Apparently he believed I could do everything my father could do. Almost immediately after my arrival on campus as an eighteen-year-old freshman, he asked me to be the regular teacher of a large Sabbath School class in the barnlike, cavernous auditorium. The classes were always jammed, with several rows of people in each. Mine was the visitor's class, and as such it never had the same people two weeks in a row.

Teaching that class was a constant struggle and terror for me in the early weeks. It was a sink-or-swim situation. I still remember the week that I studied the wrong lesson. When I realized my colossal error, I panicked. What could I do? I looked around at the people in the class and didn't see anyone who knew me. So I got up and fled. I never found out whether anyone taught the class that Sabbath.

By this time, I was fairly sure I was going to be a minister. But if that were so, I knew I couldn't quit. The continuing confidence that college professor had in me largely kept me teaching that Sabbath School class all year. I soon learned to enjoy it. So much so that I today I still love to teach whenever possible.

Soon after my graduation from college, my father became a conference president. During my early years in the ministry, I was often identified as Elder Gordon's son. Those who have seemed to live in the shadow of prominent family members can imagine how I felt the day he was introduced as Elder Gordon's father.

College taught me to teach, gave me the confidence to be a minister, and helped me to be my own self. I am grateful.

The servant of the Lord must . . . be . . . apt to teach. 2 Timothy 2:24

Paul Gordon retired in 1995 as director of the Ellen G. White Estate at the General Conference of Seventh-day Adventists in Silver Spring, Maryland. He graduated from Walla Walla College in 1952.

CANTANKEROUS TEACHER MEETS COURTEOUS CHRISTIAN *By Randy Younker*

In one of my first graduate courses in archaeology at California State University, Sacramento, my professor made it clear that he had no time for conservative Christians. He assured us that the Bible was nothing more than a compilation of folk tales that were told to children around Israelite campfires. A student sitting near me objected, saying that the Bible was the "Word of God." The professor demanded that either the student provide scientific verification for that claim or else "shut up" (his words!) for the rest of the course. The student chose the path of silence.

How was I to get along with this professor?

After class, I approached him and said I was looking forward to his course. He thanked me and asked what I did for a living. At the time, I was teaching Bible in an Adventist academy, but I certainly did not want to tell him *that*. I simply said that I was a secondary teacher. But he persisted, and I finally had to tell him I taught Bible. After a few more questions he suddenly challenged me: "You're a Seventh-day Adventist!" My face must have betrayed my shock, because he quickly assured me: "Don't worry about it. I have been teaching this course for nearly fifteen years, and the only courteous Christians I have met were Adventists." I said a silent prayer of thanks because I knew that not all Adventists are courteous. However, due to the professor's respect for those unknown Adventists, he and I were able to establish a meaningful personal relationship in the years ahead. My personal Christian outlook didn't prejudice him against me.

Some time later, some of my fellow graduate students tried to embarrass me in front of this professor by asking me if I was a creationist—which I was. Before I could answer, he came to my defense by challenging the students: "Can you conclusively prove from science that evolution is true? Because, unless you can, you had better be quiet and not bother this man!"

After my studies with this professor, I continued graduate work elsewhere and eventually became a teacher at Andrews University. Through the years, this professor has kept in touch and has visited me and my students. He has high regard for Adventist scholarship.

I have learned that personal relationships are the first step to effective witnessing.

Remind the people to be subject to rulers and authorities, to be obedient, to be ready to do whatever is good, to slander no one, to be peaceable and considerate, and to show true humility toward all men. Titus 3:1, 2, NIV

Randy Younker is assistant professor of Old Testament and biblical archaeology at the Seventh-day Adventist Theological Seminary at Andrews University in Berrien Springs, Michigan. He graduated from Pacific Union College in 1975.

HOW TO JUDGE A SPRAY CAN *By Dwight K. Nelson*

As a freshman at Southern Missionary College, I worked as a janitor in Talge Hall, the men's residence. That year we had a flu outbreak, so the dean wanted all the toilets in the dormitory disinfected. He told me I could find the disinfectant spray cans in the janitor's closet.

So I grabbed a spray can and dutifully visited every lavatory on every floor and sprayed down every toilet seat I could find.

With empty can in hand, I returned triumphantly from my mission and reported to the dean. With a quizzical look, he asked, "Did you spray all the toilet seats with *that* can?"

"Yes, sir!" I confidently acknowledged.

"Look at the can!" So I did. And to my utter chagrin, I realized that instead of picking up the disinfectant spray, I had grabbed another commercial spray can with the same white wrapper on it. The only difference was the title on the label: "Silicone Spray."

I had just sprayed every toilet seat in Talge Hall with silicone! And everybody knows that silicone is designed to ease the friction between two surfaces!

What's the moral from this hapless freshman's blunder? Simple: Never judge a spray can by its paper wrapping.

Which is true not only when you want to disinfect a dormitory, but is just as true when you want to pick a college friend or even a marriage partner. Your most lasting friendships will be with the individuals whose characters you admire and whose attractiveness is more than skin deep.

That was God's point with Samuel. Spiritual values and Christian character will far outlast a good *or* bad hair day. Sure, you want to look your best in college, but the best begins on the inside.

So when you're choosing your very best friend, go for the One with the nail scars. It's not a very photogenic portrait, but beneath the wrapping of Calvary is a love so deep and a friendship so strong that when you choose Jesus each new morning, you've got a friend who will last forever. From the inside out.

The Lord does not see as mortals see; they look on the outward appearance, but the Lord looks on the heart. 1 Samuel 16:7, NRSV

Dwight K. Nelson is senior pastor of Pioneer Memorial Church on the campus of Andrews University in Berrien Springs, Michigan. He graduated from Southern College in 1973.

A FIRST SERMON, A LOST SON, AND A PRAYER By *Charles D. Brooks*

By the time I entered college, my mother had already reached the years of unstable health. My family often heard her pray that the Lord would spare her life for two great blessings: to hear me preach and to see my missing older brother again. He had left home when I was an infant, and we had no contact with him for years. My mother prayed this prayer many times in our home.

I completed my first year of the ministerial course at Oakwood and spent the summer of 1948 at home. One afternoon, Mother and I were cleaning vegetables for canning when our pastor, Warren Banfield, drove up. He said, "Charles, I've come to see you. You will become a minister one day. I want to invite you to preach your first sermon while I am here. You take as much time as you like to prepare, and let us look forward to this experience together." With much trepidation, I chose a Sabbath six weeks off.

After the fifth week, my family received a startling message from a relative who was working on a doctorate at Columbia University. She had been to an exciting party the night before and had seen a man who bore a striking "Brooks" likeness. Incredibly, it was my long-lost brother.

He telegrammed: "Will be there Saturday."—the same day I was to preach my first sermon. Can you imagine the excitement in our home?

Sabbath morning, when I walked with the elders onto the rostrum for the service, I looked out in the congregation and saw a man, unmistakably a Brooks, with his arm around my mother. His wife (a stranger to us) was standing next to Dad. Years before, my brother had heard that Mother had died and had given up any desire to be with us because of the shock. From that Sabbath forward, he tried to compensate for the rest of his life.

My mother had prayed for two miracles. God granted both—not just the same year or week or day—but the same hour!

From this experience and others early in my college career, I learned the value—the indispensable value—of prayer to a totally loving and dependable God!! God answers prayer!

All things, whatsoever ye shall ask in prayer, believing, ye shall receive. Matthew 21:22

Charles D. Brooks is general field secretary of the General Conference of Seventh-day Adventists in Silver Spring, Maryland. He graduated from Oakwood College in 1951.

IF THERE EVER WAS A SAINT *By Lawrence T. Geraty*

Going to college for me was getting a degree and preparing for a career. Little did I realize that the thing that would stay with me the longest was the personal example and influence of my teachers.

For three years, I attended Newbold College in England while trying to convince my childhood sweetheart to marry me. Without question, the professor there who influenced my life the most was her grandfather, George D. Keough. He had previously dedicated himself to the spread of the gospel in

Egypt, where he served as a pioneer Adventist missionary. He told how he lived, as did the locals, in one-room houses without modern amenities.

He once told of a baptism down at the Nile River when a gang of angry Copts turned up to disrupt the service. Inspired with an idea that came from a flash prayer, Pastor Keough asked them how long it would have taken for the twelve apostles to baptize 3,000 new believers on the Day of Pentecost. They quickly figured that each apostle would have had to baptize 250 people, which meant if it were done in an eight-hour day, each apostle would have had to baptize a candidate every two minutes. Pastor Keough offered the gang leader his watch and said, "Now see if I can beat the apostles' record!" Before they knew it, all the new converts were baptized, and the missionary had done each one in less than two minutes!

Pastor Keough was largely self-taught and without access to many books. However, he knew large sections of the Bible and Spirit of Prophecy by heart. He started each class with a beautiful prayer and taught with a twinkle in his eye. His favorite teaching method was to juxtapose two texts that appeared to be contradictory and then proceed to show how they were complimentary. His love for the Lord was palpable. He delighted in God's Word and the treasures it contained. His greatest joy was to share God's loving character, explaining "problem texts" in harmony with that conception of God. If ever there was a saint, generations of Newbold students were convinced he was one of them.

I reached my academic goal in going to Newbold, and I got his granddaughter. In the process, I came to know Jesus and His love for me through the life, ministry, and remarkable example of Pastor George Keough.

Happy is the man who is so anxious to be with me that he watches for me daily at my gates, or waits for me outside my home! Proverbs 8:34, TLB

Lawrence T. Geraty is president of La Sierra University in Riverside, California. He graduated from Pacific Union College in 1962.

EVANGELISM VS. EXAMS *By Robert O. A. Samms*

It was an unusually special Sabbath afternoon on the campus of West Indies College, Jamaica in the late spring of 1960. Hundreds of students and faculty members gathered around a baptistry perched on the edge of the lawn overlooking the breathtaking scenes in the meadows below. Four candidates eagerly awaited baptism.

For me this was no ordinary baptism. It was freighted with great emotion. Some weeks earlier my friend, Douglas Archer, and I invited a few other students to join us in launching an evangelistic campaign in the nearby village of Albion. We pitched a tent, loaned to us by the West Jamaica Conference, on property owned by a Mr. and Mrs. Morris. Doug and I shared the preaching and the other students helped with the visitation.

We were all inexperienced. Doug was in his second college year and I was in my first. In fact, I was still completing a few college qualifying courses. Both of us had accepted the Adventist message only two years before. Though registered as a business student, I hoped to enter the ministerial course later.

Toward the end of the crusade we realized that the meeting times conflicted with our final exams at school. One Sunday I sought in vain to find even one student to accompany me to the crusade. Everybody excused themselves in order to study for exams that would begin at 7:30 the next morning.

After prayer about my problem. I felt obligated to hold the meeting, but I, too, needed to study for exams. I lit a lantern and made the long, lonely walk along the dark winding road to Albion. The meeting that night drew a big, responsive crowd and was a great success.

The following morning I wrote my history exam at 7:30 a.m. To my amazement, I got an excellent grade, despite my lack of study the evening before. In fact, I received 96 percent on the test, while the rest of the class, which had studied, fell much below. The two closest scores were 92 percent and 87 percent.

As I stood by the baptistry, I was overwhelmed by the amazing miracle of the first fruits of the evangelistic campaign and the miracle of my exam results. That experience helped to build my confidence in God and His promise to supply all our needs if we only trust Him.

Mr. and Mrs. Morris were in that first baptism. Later they donated the land where we had held the tent meeting, and we built a small chapel there. From that small beginning a thriving congregation developed.

One of my burdens is to get young Adventists involved in the church and working on their own. At only 19 years of age, I didn't have the guidance or even the direct involvement of adults. Our campaign was entirely initiated by young people. I think it's time for young Adventists to lead out in the church activities on their own initiative. Youth, take charge! God will supply all you need for success.

But my God shall supply all your need according to his riches in glory by Christ Jesus. Philippians 4:19

Robert O. A. Samms was president of the Quebec Conference of Seventh-day Adventists in Longueuil, Quebec from 1988 to 1995. He graduated from Canadian Union College in 1964.

WITH GOD IN THE
JANITOR CLOSET   *By John Kerbs*

The pungent smell of wet mops, oily dust cloths, and floor wax brings back special memories of an important forward step in my Christian life during my college years.

My attempts at a strong devotional life usually ended in frustration. Eventually I asked an older friend, "How do you do it?"

"Find a quiet place," he said. "Take your Bible, *Patriarchs and Prophets*, *Desire of Ages*, and other like books, and spend some time with God every morning before you do anything else."

I had the books, and I could make the time. Finding a quiet place in the dorm was my major problem. Then I found the janitor closet. It had lights twenty-four hours a day—quite a find in a building where the lights were out between 10:00 p.m. and 6:00 a.m. The dean gave me a key.

I used a large box of paper towels as my table and a smaller box as my chair. Surrounded by the usual elements of an institutional housekeeping operation, I spent many happy hours with God in this little space over the next couple of years. I developed a closeness with Him that I had never experienced before. In the process, I formed a life practice that has endured for more than forty years.

Keeping my devotional life simple and always in a secluded, quiet place, however unpretentious, has given me strength for each day. I've found these havens in the kitchen, the basement, under a tree in the woods, even in the bathroom. God is always there.

I have similar fond memories of a prayer room, sparsely furnished with old wicker, in the main classroom building of La Sierra College. Even today, I can still recite the words of a poem I saw often on the prayer-room wall:

> Go often to the quiet place
> Of thine own heart in prayer,
> For in the shelter of its peace,
> God is waiting there.
> Commit thyself in childlike faith
> Into His loving hand,
> Be still and know that He is God
> Who loves thee best and understands.

I recommend such a quiet time and place, however humble, as a daily part of college life, and forever.

Thou, when thou prayest, enter into thy closet, and when thou hast shut thy door, pray to thy Father which is in secret; and thy Father which seeth in secret shall reward thee openly. Matthew 6:6

John Kerbs is president of Union College in Lincoln, Nebraska. He graduated from La Sierra University in 1956.

FROM PAYDAY TO PAYDAY *By Cyril Miller*

I went to Union College without winter clothing and with only a few dollars in my pocket. I enrolled believing that God would help me find a way to make it through the year. Soon I got a job working for a drywall construction firm that was owned and operated by a childhood school friend from my hometown in Oklahoma.

When the winter came, I decided that it was best for me to find a place to work inside, where it was warm. I applied to the Nebraska state hospital and was employed at $40 per week.

During the summer after my first year, I met Marian, and we were married just a few days before school opened that fall. We managed fairly well financially, since she was working at the Adventist Book Center. We essentially covered our living and school expenses. We always put tithe and offerings at the top of our monthly list of obligations.

When we received our two small paychecks at the end of the month, we paid our tithe, tuition, rent, and grocery bill. That left us with only a few dollars to last until the next paycheck. Because those few dollars always ran out before the end of the month, a local grocery store allowed us to buy on credit.

The next year, our first baby arrived, making it difficult for Marian to work and almost impossible for us to survive on my small salary from the state hospital. I went to the personnel director and explained my situation. I told her that unless I could receive an increase in salary, I would have to look for another job.

She said, "I cannot give you a raise in your present position, because you would then be making more than other employees who have been here ten, fifteen, twenty years, or more.

"However," she continued, "I can change your classification and appoint you as an assistant director over all the male wards of the entire institution and raise your salary from $160 to $210 per month."

This was an answer to prayer. It gave me just enough money to pay our basic school and living expenses but nothing more. And amazingly, God somehow always found a way to bless that meager amount. No financial emergency ever arose.

It took a lot of faith for us to live from payday to payday with just a few dollars. But we learned a valuable lesson of trust in God's care.

I left Union College with my school bill fully paid. This experience has helped me all throughout my life. I am most thankful to God for His past, present, and future blessings!

I will bless the Lord at all times; his praise shall continually be in my mouth. Psalm 34:1, RSV

Cyril Miller is president of the Southwestern Union Conference of Seventh-day Adventists in Burleson, Texas. He graduated from Union College in 1953.

NO NEED TO BLUSH *By Robert G. Carmen*

Was I embarrassed by my religion? Was I afraid that friends, or even strangers, would make fun of my beliefs?

Those were the thoughts that rattled my brain when I enrolled as a freshman at Kent State University in Ohio.

God was clearly far from the minds of most students, who were busy with girlfriends and boyfriends, parties, and occasionally with their studies. Of course, I wanted to fit in, and my two roommates were eager to include me in their fast-paced lifestyles.

Nevertheless, I couldn't deny my faith in God. It was a simple relationship based, not on words that boomed from the pastor's pulpit, but on intensely personal experiences. I read the Bible and prayed. And I felt a wonderful peace and balance.

That first night in the dorm, as I got ready for bed, my mind raced. I usually knelt to pray before I went to sleep. It was a chance to reflect on the day—to come to terms with myself and my God.

Should I kneel tonight? I thought, with some anxiety. *What if my roommates laugh?* I could feel my face burn as I thought of the taunts I might receive. For a moment, I considered praying silently while lying in bed.

I decided to be true to myself. So I knelt, prayed, and went to bed content.

My nightly prayers did not go unnoticed; my roommates rather enjoyed poking fun at me. I sensed they would never understand.

Late one night, both roommates stumbled into the room, very drunk. One was having problems making it to his bed, so I got up to help him.

"All right, you can lie down now," I said.

He looked at me seriously. "No," he said, "I have to say my prayers first." It was a sincere comment. While I was sad to see him drunk, the alcohol had obviously removed the walls that normally kept him from revealing any interest in God or prayer. I knew then that at some deep inner level, my prayers had influenced his thoughts and had stirred him to contemplate his own spiritual journey.

I don't know what has happened to my roommate since then. But I still pray every night, and I'm not embarrassed to pray in restaurants or any other public place—because I know that people *do* notice. My simple influence might help someone, somewhere experience the same joy I've found in my relationship with God.

In thee, O Lord, do I put my trust; let me never be ashamed: deliver me in thy righteousness. Psalm 31:1

Robert G. Carmen is president of Southern California Healthcare Network in Glendale, California. He graduated from Loma Linda University in 1969.

DISASTER AT MIDTERM *By Penny Estes Wheeler*

One of my biggest problems during my first year at Andrews University was Western Civilization. By that, I mean the academic class, of course—not the idea.

History, to me, was a hodgepodge of people I'd never heard of and of places I couldn't visualize. I'd never learned how to study for history, and it seemed that no matter how hard I tried, I missed two or three questions on those stupid "nickel quizzes" the teacher, Clarence Richardson, popped with great regularity.

To compound the problem, the class met at 7:30 a.m. Oh, I usually made it—without breakfast, of course, and often with just brushing my teeth, yanking on some clothes, and dashing across campus to Griggs Hall. Then again, sometimes I'd never hear the alarm clock at all.

I became worried as the midterm exam loomed closer. I made a determined effort to study harder, organize better, memorize more. And I actually began to improve on the pop quizzes. But I knew I had to do well on the midterm if I was going to have a decent grade.

I stayed up studying until very late the night before the exam. Not surprisingly, I slept through the alarm and all the way through that first-period class and the midterm exam.

I woke up in a panic. I figured I had one single, terrible option. I could go to our kind young teacher and throw myself on his mercy. Of course, I could think of a dozen good reasons why he should throw me out of his office or tell me that he'd just average my quiz scores for my final grade.

I stood in the hallway outside his cubbyhole office, working up my nerve. Then I sort of tiptoed through Mr. Richardson's doorway and began a garbled account of late-night study, high hopes, and disaster.

He looked at me with a smile and asked if I was going to sleep through any more classes. Then we set up a time for me to come to his office and take the exam.

Mercy. Forgiveness. Totally undeserved grace.

Something like what Christ grants to me even yet.

All have sinned and fall short of the glory of God, and are justified freely by his grace through the redemption that came by Christ Jesus. Romans 3:23, 24, NIV

Penny Estes Wheeler is editor of Women of Spirit *at the Review and Herald Publishing Association in Hagerstown, Maryland. She graduated from Andrews University in 1967.*

THE SMOTHERING PILLOW *By Lonnie Melashenko*

Worry is as American as apple pie and Chevrolet. We are a nation of worriers. Observe it in the classroom with the new teacher. Feel it in the squeezed study of the medical student as she crams for her exams. Sense it in the airport departure lounge as parents wave goodbye to a son leaving for combat duty.

Young adolescents worry the most: My school performance. My looks. How well others like me.

The legacy of worry can be painful. Especially during test week. After crunching for finals at La Sierra University one semester, I awoke with a start. I dreamed I'd picked up my American History exam, stared at the blue booklet, and blanked out. I worried about the test so much I couldn't remember anything I studied, so in my dream I handed in my paper without writing a word!

Worry is a collision emotion that can leave you crippled. It smothers our pleasant dreams by placing a pillow over our faith. Worry can strap a short leash on your vision and teach you to roll over and play dead when scary statistics and pessimistic reports snap their fingers.

Jesus knew life stressors cause us worry. Things. Relationships. Money.

He had a simple remedy. Trust. "What does worrying get you, Lon?" He asks. Nothing!

"I'm not *worrying*, I'm *planning!*" I protest. But there is a difference. Planning produces a sense of security. Worry is self-destructive. It is borrowing trouble. Yet I often prime the pump of worry before I even pick up the morning paper. I burn up all sorts of energy lying awake as my mind runs up and down the dark alleys of imaginary dread.

The remedy for worry is trust. I get rid of worry the same way I stay in a dentist's chair: TRUST. I consciously choose and willfully abandon self to Someone higher who is trustworthy.

When I am afraid [worried], I put my trust in thee. Psalm 56:3, RSV. Worrying about whether or not you'll always have enough to wear won't change a thing. So why worry? Matthew 6:28, The Clear Word

Lonnie Melashenko is speaker/director of the Voice of Prophecy radio broadcast in Simi Valley, California. He graduated from La Sierra University in 1968.

HOW A BORING GENERAL CONFERENCE PREACHER HELPED ME MEET MY WIFE *By Charles J. Griffin*

"When you find beauty, brains, and piety all wrapped up in the same package, Willie, you ought to take an armload of it."

That was the counsel of M. D. Lewis, my college Bible professor. Besides the choice lifework, the matter of choosing a life companion has to be one of the most important decisions many students make during college days. As a young theology major at Southwestern Junior College, I took seriously Ellen White's counsel that young people contemplating marriage should pray twice as much as they normally do.

One weekend, a group of nursing students came from Porter Hospital in Denver to promote the nursing program. While this doubtless was an important event for some of the fellows on campus, it was no big deal for me. Of course, at chapel I had seen those neat-looking girls with their stiffly starched nursing uniforms and their dark blue capes with the red inner liners thrown smartly back over their shoulders. But so what! I didn't know any of them anyway.

On Sabbath, the treasurer from the General Conference was scheduled to preach. As a budding preacher myself, I had a less-than-wholesome regard for preachers from the General Conference. They usually were particularly boring—especially treasurers. So I chose to pass up attending the college church, with the General Conference dignitary, and presumably all those nurses from Porter. Instead, I went with Elder Lewis, my Bible teacher, to the small church in nearby Cleburne, where he was to give the sermon.

When we arrived at the church, I didn't notice that one of those nursing students from Colorado was standing there. She apparently looked me over with approval. Later, during the service, she decided that I might be a Mormon, because I didn't sing the songs and was studying a strange-looking little black book (my Greek New Testament, to impress my teacher).

When church was over, Elder Lewis greeted the members as they filed out. The nursing student came by, and Elder Lewis said, "Let me introduce you to Charles Griffin, a theology student from the college."

A simple moment of encounter at college? No, more than that. After more than thirty years of ministry on three separate continents, Evelyn and I understand the importance of that meeting on Sabbath. We know it was providential. Christian education, if it does nothing else but settle the question of a life companion, is worth the investment.

Trust in the Lord with all thine heart. . . . In all thy ways acknowledge him, and he shall direct thy paths. Proverbs 3:5, 6

Charles J. Griffin is president of the Greater New York Conference of Seventh-day Adventists in Manhasset, New York. He graduated from Union College in 1961.

THIRTY SECONDS EQUALS
NINETEEN YEARS *By Robert J. Kloosterhuis*

It was a beautiful spring day in my junior year, the kind of day I would much rather spend outside enjoying the sun than inside a classroom watching fluorescent lights blink. Homiletics class droned along with a score and a half of my fellow students critiquing each other about platform performance and delivery.

Near the end of the period, Barry, a senior ministerial student, slipped into class and with noticeable animation whispered something to the teacher seated not far from me.

At an opportune moment, the teacher announced that Barry had just received a call from the General Conference to go to Africa as a missionary. It electrified the class. Prospects for ministerial internships were practically nonexistent. During those years, more college graduates were accepted as medical students at Loma Linda University, alone, than were hired as ministerial interns throughout the whole North American Division.

I listened with rapt attention as Barry related details about the call, what his responsibilities would be, and when he and his family would leave. I became very excited about his call and thought, *Oh, what an opportunity that would be.*

As he related more details, I thought about my own future. What would I be looking forward to next year at this time, with graduation just a couple of months away? Would there be a call? Right then, while still listening to Barry, I turned my thoughts heavenward and prayed a short, focused prayer. I told God that I would be willing to accept a call to the mission field and would consider such an invitation an honor. My conversation with God beneath those blinking fluorescent lights took no longer than thirty seconds.

Before that time, I had given mission service a few respectful, fleeting moments of consideration. But on that day I felt overwhelmed by a desire to serve the Lord in some mission land. And so I prayed that prayer.

In the following twelve months, I didn't reflect much on that commitment, though I did fill out a mission-service application form and mail it to the General Conference.

About six months before graduation, I received a telephone call from the General Conference Secretariat inquiring if my wife and I would be willing to serve in Haiti. Yes, we would be willing. Forty-five days after graduation, my wife, our six-week-old baby boy, and I landed in Port-au-Prince. Little did we realize at the time that we had begun nineteen years of exciting mission service.

It all started that day in homiletics class when I prayed fervently for God to lead in my life. That simple request has proved to me many, many times since that God delights to fulfill our requests—even thirty-second prayers.

Delight yourself in the Lord and he will give you the desires of your heart. Psalm 37:4, NIV

Robert J. Kloosterhuis is general vice president of the General Conference of Seventh-day Adventists in Silver Spring, Maryland, and chairman of the board of Andrews University. He graduated from Andrews University in 1954.

SPONSORED BY GOD *By Sali Jo Hand*

While recovering from the cataclysmic shock of an unexpected divorce, I was called by God to the ministry. My parents agreed to support me and my children until I completed my undergraduate degree. Confident of God's leading and care, I headed for Union College. For two exciting years, I studied hard, worked part time, and mothered full time. By God's grace, I balanced the staggering load of Greek, art, and theology classes; curling my hair; and keeping my boys fed, clothed, and read to.

When we were ready to graduate, almost all of my male classmates in theology had been sponsored by some conference to attend seminary. Every conference president who had interviewed me had said, "You are obviously gifted and called by God to ministry. But we can't sponsor you to seminary because we can't ordain you. Policy doesn't allow us to sponsor anyone we can't ordain."

At the end of these discouraging interviews, God always seemed to say, "Don't worry. I've called you. I'll take care of you."

Eager to go to seminary and begin work on my M.Div., I loaded up my kids, dog, bird, and our belongings in a U-Haul truck and headed for Berrien Springs, Michigan. I had only one major problem. My parents' support ended August 31. After that, I was on my own. I soon learned that I couldn't work to support my family, mother my children, and successfully complete an M.Div. all at the same time. Other potential options for income quickly vanished. I looked to God for help, trusting His promise: "My God will supply every need of yours" (Philippians 4:19, RSV). By August's end, I would have no job, no money, three kids, and a B.A. in art and theology. I was headed for financial disaster unless God performed a miracle.

In my life, it seems that God always takes me right to the edge before He intervenes. Two days before the last day of August, I received by certified mail a cashier's check for $17,800 from an unexpected inheritance. When I figured it all out, I realized that this was the exact amount I would have received at that time as a sponsored seminary student.

I felt I had been overlooked and set aside by every SDA conference in North America, but I was not overlooked by my Father in heaven. I was sponsored to go to seminary by God Himself. It doesn't get any better than that!

My God will supply every need of yours. Philippians 4:19

Sali Jo Hand is director of youth ministries of the Potomac Conference of Seventh-day Adventists in Staunton, Virginia. She graduated from Union College in 1987.

NOWHERE TO GO *By Thomas G. Bunch*

There it was—Black Mountain—rising majestically above us into the clear, deep blue sky! My Wilderness Ecology class took me on a week-long backpacking trip into the Marble Mountains of northern California. We had hiked through the native forest, endured the switchbacks, and broke out at timberline. Suddenly, the black marble peak towered over us a thousand feet above.

After lecturing on the ecology around us, our instructor allowed us a couple of hours to explore the area or climb to the peak of Black Mountain. My hiking buddy and I decided to follow a natural trail at the base of a cliff. Young and reckless, we inched our way along this narrow trail, which soon was no longer at the base of the cliff. Soon we were some forty feet high, and our trail was vanishing under rock slides. We were stuck to the side of the cliff with nowhere to go. Gripping the wall frantically with our hands, we knew we were in serious trouble. We earnestly hoped that just around the next bulge of rock we could find an escape route.

Immediately, many thoughts, questions, and promises crowded my mind. *Why didn't we stay with the main group? I will never do anything stupid again. I want to be home with my brother and parents! Lord, if You just get me out of this mess, I will serve You the rest of my life!*

After the thoughts came the prayers. No bargains now, just, "Lord, help us get out of this predicament." After what seemed like hours, we decided that hanging on a cliff wasn't productive. Soon we began carefully and painstakingly reversing our direction, inch by inch, back to our starting point. At last, we made it. We were delighted to get back to safety and be reunited with the rest of our class.

Whenever I think of this incident, I am reminded of the vision Ellen White recorded in *Life Sketches,* pages 190 to 193. There, she describes the journey to heaven where the trail gets so steep and narrow that the saints are on the brink of despair. Suddenly, cords hang down the cliff, which the saints grab and use for safe traveling to heaven.

Oh, how we could have used those cords that day on Black Mountain! Or maybe we *were* held safe to the mountain by invisible heavenly cords. Each day of my life, I need to make sure I am holding on securely to that heavenly cord—our Saviour Jesus, the One who can help us safely reach the top of the mountain.

Thomas G. Bunch is dean of students and assistant academic vice president for records of Southwestern Adventist College in Keene, Texas. He graduated from Pacific Union College in 1966.

SALVATION AND THE
STUDENT ASSOCIATION *By Steve Willsey*

Weeks of Prayer made little impact on me until the spring of my junior year. E. L. Minchin from the General Conference Youth Department came to Andrews University, where I was a student. Speaking in his rich Australian accent and with years of experience in youth work, Minchin presented the gospel in a way that changed my life.

My own spiritual journey had consisted of trying to be good but keeping my distance from God. During that one week, God began a work that eventually led me to change my career plans from hospital administration to the ministry. Only a beginning was made during that Week of Prayer; it was two years later that I made the formal change in career plans and twenty more years before I was able to find full assurance of my salvation through faith in Jesus Christ.

A more immediate consequence of Elder Minchin's Week of Prayer was the quality of leadership I gave as president of the Student Association that year. I called the Student Senate together and told them of the change in my life. I appealed for them, also, to consider a partnership with Jesus. Some of my friends laughed, but I was completely serious. Instead of confronting the school administration on some issues that concerned us that year, the Student Association took a more cooperative position and met our goals with much less pain.

I'm thankful there is much greater emphasis now on salvation by faith. All I knew was righteousness by my own works. Until I heard Elder Minchin, Jesus only seemed to be against me rather than someone whom I could love and trust. Elder Minchin planted the seed of trust in the Lord, which is now in full blossom in my life.

It is by grace you have been saved, through faith—and this not from yourselves, it is the gift of God—not by works, so that no one can boast. Ephesians 2:8, 9, NIV

Steve Willsey is associate pastor of the Spencerville Seventh-day Adventist Church in Spencerville, Maryland. He graduated from Andrews University in 1961.

SINGING IN HARMONY *By Raj Attiken*

Music and people. Why I was impressed with these ordinary elements of life, I do not know.

My first impression upon arriving at college was of the great diversity among students and faculty. I had come to college having had some exposure to diversity. But here, for the first time, I was immersed in a population from many cultures and national origins. Here were people who dressed differently, who enjoyed foods I didn't even know were edible, whose language and dialects were foreign, and who had habits, customs, and ways of doing things that seemed strange to me.

I experienced what I have since come to know as a "reality immersion." I was introduced to the fact that God's creative and redemptive activity spans the globe in many rich, colorful, and imaginative ways.

During those early weeks and months at college, I was forced to relate to the reality of diversity. How does one learn to understand, accept, and appreciate differences?

One helpful lesson came to me in the form of music. When the students met for worship or chapel, they sang in harmony; they sang in parts. I began to love the sounds of harmony. I was impressed that people of diverse backgrounds and ethnicity could sing in harmony and that when they do, they produce wonderful music! If these people could also *live* in harmony, they could make their world a beautiful place. I learned that in order to resolve two dissonant notes, one can either force the notes together until they make the sounds one wants to hear or one can add a third note, which will resolve the dissonance into consonance. From the sounds of harmonious music on that campus, I learned that despite our differences, we can celebrate our harmony in life through many joyful, creative, and imaginative ways. To force others to think, act, and be like us would deny the very nature of our creation and redemption.

My early days in college taught me that the future belongs to those who can add the right notes to life.

All of you who were baptized "into" Christ have put on the family likeness of Christ. Gone is the distinction between Jew and Greek, slave and free man, male and female—you are all one in Christ Jesus. Galatians 3:27, 28, Phillips, revised edition

Raj Attiken is secretary of the Ohio Conference of Seventh-day Adventists in Mount Vernon, Ohio. He graduated from Spicer Memorial College in Pune, India, in 1971.

LOVING GOD
WITH ALL MY MIND
By Humberto M. Rasi

The change of pace from my easygoing academy days to the bracing experience of college was dramatic. I had enrolled in an intensive program at our Adventist college in Argentina, a program especially designed for those intending to pursue advanced studies in a public university. Gone was the leisurely tempo of my secondary studies. Instead, I was confronted with demanding courses that explored critically the broad fields of philosophy, history, science, religion, and theology.

Fortunately, my experience was guided by a superb group of teachers who not only had mastered their subjects, but who also approached them from a committed biblical perspective. Although I did not know it at the time, they taught me how Christians can love God—as Jesus stated it—with all our mind (see Mark 12:30). In other words, they helped me to think *Christianly*.

This attitude toward God and knowledge, which I have sought to apply in my personal and professional life, has three dimensions:

Humility. The Christian mind acknowledges that God is both our Creator and the source of all true knowledge (see Proverbs 1:7). Our point of reference is the Bible. We stand in awe at the incredible complexity and magnificent variety of God's universe. The more we learn about His creation, the more we want to worship and obey Him with all our being.

Excitement. To apply our mind to any field of knowledge is to begin probing into the very mind of God. Wherever we look into the cosmos, in spite of the Fall, we can trace the plans of a Designer who is attentive to detail and a lover of beauty. When we study the products of human creativity, we know that if they are noble, they reflect somehow God's perfect goodness (see James 1:17).

Wisdom. Beyond knowledge, the Christian mind seeks wisdom. Based on God's principles, we wish to form correct plans to achieve the desired results—on this earth and beyond. We want to make wise decisions in the practical aspects of life: selecting a career, choosing our spouse, spending our free time, investing our resources.

In this lifelong search, we are greatly encouraged by knowing that we are not alone—the Holy Spirit is ready to guide us "into all truth" (John 16:13) until we meet God face to face.

You shall love the Lord your God with all your heart, and with all your soul, and with all your mind, and with all your strength. Mark 12:30, RSV

Humberto M. Rasi is director of education of the General Conference of Seventh-day Adventists in Silver Spring, Maryland. He graduated from River Plate Adventist College in 1954.

LET'S WAIT AND SEE By William Loveless

Wait and see is the perfect performance formula for a procrastinator in denial. It could also be an effective style of leadership.

I learned the importance of waiting and seeing from Leon B. Losey, dean of men, leader of young men, and grower of world-class flowers (irises) at Walla Walla College.

A careful, taciturn man, Losey spoke few words and conveyed to his dormitory men—and we all knew we were his men—a deep sense of pride at being the men of Omicron Pi Sigma.

If there was any way possible, I knew the dean would be on my side. He told me so more than once and demonstrated it more often than that. I had arrived on campus from California, the land of fruits and nuts, as I was told by classmates almost immediately after settling into Sittner Hall, room 135.

In those days, the lights went out at 10:30 in the dorm, and in the evening, we signed in and out of the library and the dormitory. My roommate and I managed to thread an electric cord through the radiator pipe into the next room, which was a laundry room with all-night lights. Against the rules? Yes. Did the dean know within days after we rigged up our neat arrangement? Yes. Did the dean say anything? No. Did we think we were wise guys who had fooled the dean? Yes. Wait and see.

On our wing of Sittner, the shower across the hall was separate from the toilets. To enter the shower, one had to step over a four-inch threshold of tile. On Friday evening, what a wonderful wading pool the shower became after we had blocked up the drains with washcloths and filled the room with hot water four inches deep. Never mind leaks through the minute holes in the tile, water in the hall, and depleted hot water supply for men seeking a shower after our water sport. Poor judgment? Yes. Did the dean know? Wait and see.

It was when I suffered the loss of my large travel suitcase that I saw the dean at his best. I had stored my suitcase in the "trunk room," as the dean called it. Locked most of the time, the room had been entered during a rare time when it was unlocked, and my fine suitcase had disappeared. I reported the loss to the dean, who registered concern and promised, "I'll keep it in mind, Bill." Meanwhile, "Wait and see."

A month later, he brought the suitcase to my room. He had found it hidden under an old mattress in another building. Relieved, I readily responded to his invitation to "talk for a minute." We both sat down. "That electric cord," he said, pointing knowingly at the offending member. "You need to retract that from the laundry room. And by the way, Bill, could you lend your influence to eliminate the pool parties in the shower on your wing of the dorm?"

So he had known all the time but was waiting to see what would develop. He was willing to wait on a young man growing up. He saw the foolishishness, but beyond that, he saw what we were becoming, and that's what gave impetus to his dormitory leadership.

I remember with great warmth some compliments and encouragement from the dean when I pursued more meaningful projects. And sometime later, when the girl I asked to marry me consulted with Dean Losey about my merits, his answers to her were in my favor. I'm thankful this man, a person of exemplary character, was willing to "wait and see."

Yet the Lord is waiting to be merciful to you. He is ready to take pity on you because he always does what is right. Happy are those who put their trust in the Lord. Isaiah 30:18, TEV

William Loveless is senior pastor of Loma Linda University Church in Loma Linda, California. He graduated from Walla Walla College in 1949.

DISCOVERING GOD'S PLAN *By Alvin Goulbourne*

As a ministerial student at Oakwood College, I sometimes questioned my calling. However, I paid careful attention to the professors who encouraged us to give Bible studies and to pray for the sick.

One summer I worked in Texas as a student colporteur, selling the book *Guide to Better Living*. At one home, I met a woman who was very interested in the book but said she couldn't afford to buy it. Her husband had recently had a stroke, and the doctors said there was nothing more that they could do for him. They sent home to die. I prayed with her for the healing of her husband, telling her that there is nothing too hard for the Lord. Leaving the book with the woman, I told her to follow the health instructions it contained and said I would return for another visit.

Whenever I got the chance in the days ahead, I stopped by that home and prayed for the healing of the husband. Then, for three or four weeks, I was away working in another area. When I returned, the man wasn't home, and I feared the worst, thinking that he had died. When I found his wife, she told me she had been following the instructions in the book I left with her. Her husband was out on a fishing trip with a friend. We praised God together.

This experience of answered prayer and healing helped me to realize that the Lord did have a special work for me to do. I no longer questioned my calling. It was then that I realized that God could and would use me as a messenger of hope to the downcast, the sick, and those carrying burdens. I learned that man's extremity can be God's opportunity to show His strength, power, and love. Ministry for me is more than preaching. It also involves teaching faith in God's abilities, teaching hope in knowing that He keeps His promises, and helping others to learn to do His will.

Trust in the Lord with all thine heart; and lean not unto thine own understanding. In all thy ways acknowledge him, and he shall direct thy paths. Proverbs 3:5, 6.

Alvin Goulbourne is secretary of the Atlantic Union Conference of Seventh-day Adventists in South Lancaster, Massachusetts. He graduated from Oakwood College in 1951.

IF AT FIRST YOU DON'T SUCCEED, BEG FOR MERCY By James A. Cress

There was no question about it: I was called to be a writer and to a brilliant literary career.

I arrived at Southern College's freshmen orientation full of confidence. After the formality of a qualifying exam, I expected to enroll in Evlyn Lindberg's all-important honors composition class.

Certainly, I was eligible. I was an English major, along with theology. In academy I had worked as assistant to the head English teacher and written a monthly column for the academy newspaper. My scores on various verbal-skill assessments were always high, and I had worked in the print shop as a typesetter. Furthermore, my best friends, a year or so ahead of me, were now the literary elite of the college campus. With such background and connections, surely I was destined to edit the college newspaper.

The word around the English department was that you didn't have the right stuff to pursue an English major if you couldn't make at least an A- in the toughest class a beginning writer would ever encounter. Of course, I wasn't afraid of the teacher, even if others rightly were. This classic Scandinavian spinster with two middle names and a reputation for severity that withered triviality was no terror for me. I was eager to have her red pen address my compositions.

Her class would launch my writing career. After all, I was also a theology major. So my first job offer out of college would at least be for a staff position on the *Youth's Instructor*. Accepting that job would only be necessary if there were no openings at the moment on the editorial staff of the *Review and Herald*.

The morning after taking the qualifying exam, I sauntered over to see the posted results. I looked forward to seeing my student ID number and score at or near the top of the list of those accepted into the privileged class. But something was terribly wrong. My name wasn't near the top. In fact, it wasn't on the list at all. If this list was accurate, I had failed to qualify. Failure was not in my universe. Worse, how could I ever face my peers if I were excluded from the inner circle.

There must be a mistake. I checked with the department secretary. The list was complete. My score was accurate. I was devastated.

I just had to get into that class. Mustering whatever courage I had left, I made an appointment with this intimidating professor I now very much feared. Would there be a waiting list? Did she ever make an exception? Would she expand the class size? The lump in my throat had grown to a brick by the time I faced PROFESSOR OF ENGLISH, EVLYN MARIA MATILDA LINDBERG.

Wonder of wonders. I received mercy. Marvelous miracle—at least for my fragile self-image—she would make an exception to allow me to try to keep up with the others. Mercy was mingled with justice, however. She took me into the class, but that was the only slack she ever gave me.

And what of my literary career? I never edited the college newspaper. The *Youth's Instructor* not only failed to call, it folded. To this day, I've never been called to the editorial staff of any magazine. The *Adventist Re-*

view has published an article or two that I've written, and I do have to prepare a monthly column for *Ministry* by deadline.

But the greatest lesson I learned in Freshman Composition was not about grammar or style, syntax or structure. The greatest lesson I learned came when a wise and generous woman extended grace to me instead of the results of my own works. *I didn't get what I deserved.*

By grace are ye saved . . . not of works, lest any man should boast. Ephesians 2:8, 9

James A. Cress is secretary of the Ministerial Association of the General Conference of Seventh-day Adventists in Silver Spring, Maryland. He graduated from Southern College in 1971.

ABOVE BOARD–SORT OF *By Steve Case*

Frequently in Scripture God describes His relationship with us as a romance between lovers. If this is true, the college experience has much to teach us about our relationship with God.

It was all very much above board—sort of. She was still in academy when I went away to college. We broke up so both of us could date around, which was a good thing, since I now had exposure to a entirely new crop of coeds on the comparatively large college campus. A trip home once a month, however, "kept the fires burning" on that front.

I didn't really seek the second relationship. Both of us were on the gymnastics team. Our schedules meshed quite nicely. We became friends, nothing more (for a while). But good romantic relationships often start as "just friends." She never asked about any attachments I might have back home.

Everything worked fine until the academy girl paid a surprise visit one Sabbath. Yes, I was very surprised to see her! I dashed her up to the corner of the balcony at church, since "those were the best seats" and "we wouldn't get them if we hung around the lobby and saw a bunch of people." After church I threw together a few things for an impromptu picnic—a chance for just the two of us to be together without interruptions from others.

My quick thinking and deft maneuvering worked until later that afternoon, when our path crossed hers. In such a situation, three is definitely a crowd! I received a "Dear John" letter from the (former) academy sweetheart. The college "friend" told me she had her own academy beau back home. Our romance ended, and the friendship faded.

How could everything blow up in my face when I had been above board with this whole thing—sort of? In spite of attempted coverups and withholding pertinent information, I fooled myself into believing I was basically transparent. I ignored the telltale signals of panicked attempts to prevent the three of us from ever being together. I had reasons for all of this, some even based on compassion to not hurt anyone! What a joke.

Polygamy definitely wouldn't work for me. "Poly-dating" certainly didn't. And there's no reason to believe it would work in my relationship with God. Rationalizing that God is simply "an important part of one's life" falls short of having no other gods. To what extent are other things denying you quality time with God? Are things really above board with you and God?

I, the Lord your God, am very possessive. I will not share your affection with any other god! Exodus 20:5, TLB

Steve Case is president of Piece of the Pie Ministries in Sacramento, California. He graduated from Pacific Union College in 1980.

WHAT GOD WANTS ME TO DO *By Herb Broeckel*

I can't remember a time when I didn't feel God wanted me to be a minister.

Mother raised us with stories about the years that Dad was a pastor/ evangelist. In our daily worships, she often included ideas about what God wanted to do through us. My older brother became a doctor. My sister became a nurse. All through academy and into college, I knew I would be a minister.

One day, when I was a junior theology major walking under the "Gateway to Service" arch at Columbia Union College, the terrible thought hit me: *Was I taking theology to fulfill my father's uncompleted church career and my mother's prayers? Or was the ministry really for me?*

This became an agonizing question in my mind. I've generally been among that lucky group of people who fall asleep almost before their head hits the pillow. Staying awake half the night praying was a new experience for me, but I had to find some resolution to my quandary. No one on campus had any idea of the huge struggle I was going through. It took several weeks of late-night conversations with God, but I eventually found great freedom and confidence in my call. I didn't turn from my childhood training. I finished my theology degree and became a pastor.

I discovered that fulfilling the text below means that whatever path my career takes, I fulfill my childhood training when I follow God's call, wherever that leads me. Ever since those sleepless weeks during my junior year in college, I've known that I was doing what God wants me to do.

Proverbs 22:6 has been fulfilled in my life in unexpected and wonderful ways. When I turned to Him He gave direction to guide me through college and ever since, I have continued to turn to Him. I can talk to God about anything. I have found that responding to God's influence provides a lifetime of blessing.

Train a child in the way he should go, and when he is old he will not turn from it. Proverbs 22:6, NIV

Herb Broeckel is president of the Potomac Conference of Seventh-day Adventists in Staunton, Virginia. He graduated from Columbia Union College in 1959.

THE DISCOVERY CHANNEL *By John W. Fowler*

Sweat beaded on my forehead. It soaked the palms of my hands and discolored my shirt. Freshman Comp was a terror. One class period I would face a ten-point quiz; the next allowed me only fifteen minutes to write a three-hundred-word essay. Study. Memorization. Worry. Sweat. No matter how hard I tried, I failed. Simply believing God wanted me in college didn't compensate for having only one year of regular high-school credit.

I had been converted to Adventism and called to the ministry at age twenty-three. A General Equivalency Diploma (GED) gained my acceptance to Southern College. What I knew formally about the English language could be written on a scrap of paper and fit into a small thimble. After the third disastrous class period, when everyone had left the classroom, I approached Miss Lindberg and pleaded for help.

"I have no doubt that you can do the work," she assured me, "but it will require faith, disciplined effort, and time."

"Our minds," Miss Lindberg continued, "were created by God with unlimited understanding. However, the mind is like a muscle in your arm or leg. It weakens if not used; but with exercise it grows strong and powerful."

To pass the next quiz, she recommended that I begin my study with prayer. Then she advised that I read the first paragraph of the assigned story as many times as necessary until I could recall the narrative line as well as the facts and details. The first paragraph thus mastered, I could go on to the second and following paragraphs in the same fashion.

That evening, the Lord and I took my mind to task. It balked, argued, and threatened. After two hours of disciplined, concentrated, and painful thought, mixed with sweat and prayer, my mind grudgingly copied the first paragraph in my memory file.

After four hours, I had the entire story firmly recorded in my mind. I could even turn my thoughts to other subjects and back again to the story, recalling it at will.

On the next quiz, I scored 100 percent! I couldn't believe it. I was ecstatic. My life was changed forever. I completed Freshman Comp with the second-highest accumulated score in the class, earning an "A" both semesters. My graduating class gave me the honor of serving as its president. Impossible? Nothing is with Christ.

I can do all things through Jesus Christ who strengtheneth me. Philippians 4:13

John W. Fowler is executive secretary of the Kentucky-Tennessee Conference of Seventh-day Adventists in Goodlettsville, Tennessee. He graduated from Southern College in 1964.

RECONCILED BY BLOOD *By Juan R. Rivera*

In 1967, I enrolled at Montemorelos University in Mexico. Felipe, an education major, gave the new students from the United States a very warm welcome and was active in assisting us. He was cordial and very friendly.

Not long after, things began to change with Felipe. He lost his interest in helping us. He was not the fellow I had met earlier in the school year. He became bitter, hateful, and rude. My presence apparently so antagonized him that he insulted and verbally abused me. I tried to be kind and courteous. After all, what is a future minister for the Seventh-day Adventist Church expected to do? The days went by, and Felipe's attitude and actions against me became unbearable.

One night while I was sleeping, he placed a dirty wet mop on my face. I awoke scared and humiliated and heard him laughing all the way to his room. I didn't know what to do. I asked God to help me bear this ugly situation.

One afternoon, I saw Felipe cutting tall weeds with a big machete. I could tell he was exhausted. His back was toward me, and as I approached to tap him on the shoulder to offer my help, he turned around swinging his long knife. I was not able to pull my hand back fast enough. I felt a sharp pain, and not wanting to look at my injury, I folded my arm. But Felipe rushed over and pulled my arm out to see what had happened. When he saw bones and ligaments exposed, he was stunned.

He hugged me and with tears began to beg me to forgive him. I assured him that it was an accident and that everything would be all right.

Indeed, everything did turn out all right. From that day, Felipe and I established a very close and unique friendship. Praise God, we were reconciled.

Having made peace through the blood of his cross . . . [he] reconcile[d] all things unto himself. Colossians 1:20

Juan R. Rivera is secretary of the Central California Conference of Seventh-day Adventists in Clovis, California. He graduated from La Sierra University in 1972.

YOU CAN'T LOSE WITH JESUS *By Trevor H. C. Baker*

I was a newly baptized Seventh-day Adventist, and I was moving up rapidly in my banking job. Then suddenly, I found myself forced to choose between my job and my God. Sabbath problems shattered the comfort I was enjoying in my promising career.

At the time, I could not understand why I had to experience these problems when my Adventist friends in similar jobs were free of them.

Later, I realized that, like the prophet Jonah, I was settling comfortably into that career as an escape from a nagging consciousness deep inside that beckoned me to a different line of work: the gospel ministry.

The ensuing months after quitting my banking job were difficult. There were no offers of employment and countless refusals. After much prayer and agonizing and of questioning God, I decided to respond to the quiet promptings of the Holy Spirit. I enrolled in Oakwood College.

I arrived at the college with a total of $600 to my name and no promise or prospect of help from any source. I soon discovered that my money would be gone by the end of the first semester. My years in college were years of study, work, and constant uncertainty whether my account would be cleared to take exams at the end of each term.

On one such occasion, when my account typically was too high, I went to the student accounts office to plead my case. To my utter surprise, I learned that my bill had been paid. To this day, I know not how or by whom it was paid; but I am confident that when God and His will are placed first in our lives, He takes care of His own.

Seek ye first the kingdom of God, and his righteousness; and all these things shall be added unto you. Matthew 6:33

Trevor H. C. Baker is executive secretary of the Northeastern Conference of Seventh-day Adventists in Jamaica, New York. He graduated from Oakwood College in 1967.

NAVY LESSONS   *By Clint Kreitner*

I arrived at the United Stated Naval Academy thinking I was pretty hot stuff. I had been at the top of my high-school class academically, the class president, and the recipient of four all-expenses-paid college scholarships. I was ready to set the world straight.

Soon, however, Spiritual Lesson Number One confronted me. I was forced to learn that it is much easier to be a big fish in a small pond than in a big pond. I had come from a small-town high-school class of ninety-one students. What a shock it was to be swallowed up in a college that had chosen approximately one thousand freshmen from a nationwide applicant pool of over twenty thousand! Within two grading periods, I became painfully aware of how challenging it would be for me even to stay in the top 20 percent of the class. The spiritual concept of humility became very real!

"Do not think of yourself more highly than you ought, but think of yourself with sober judgment in accordance with the measure of faith God has given you" (Romans 12:3, NEV).

Forty-one years later, I realize that my initial brashness resulted from my undeveloped faith. I also came to understand that God's intent was to gently, yet persistently expose me to a carefully planned curriculum of spiritual lessons.

Spiritual Lesson Number Two during those four years at Annapolis presented itself in a manner that, from a religious perspective, is quite implicit. Yet the concept comes straight from the Scriptures: teamwork.

My training as a midshipman engendered in me a passionate commitment to teamwork. This concept was drilled into us in many ways: in the Dilbert Dunker drill, where we were strapped tightly into a simulated airplane cockpit, sent down a track, and turned upside down under water; in flying off an aircraft carrier in a navy jet fighter; by participating in an amphibious landing (in which I would have drowned had it not been for an alert classmate).

From these rigorous exercises, I quickly learned about dependence upon others. I now understand that teamwork and dependence are rooted in the biblical doctrine of the spiritual gifts.

As a health ministry leader today, I cherish the spiritual lessons God taught me at the United States Naval Academy.

Just as each of us has one body with many members, and these members do not all have the same function, so in Christ we who are many form one body and each member belongs to all the others. Romans 12:4, 5, NEV

Clint Kreitner is president and chief executive officer of Reading Rehabilitation Hospital in Reading, Pennsylvania. He graduated from the United States Naval Academy in 1958.

GENETIC TERROR   *By Gary Patterson*

I t was common knowledge on the Walla Walla College campus, where I arrived as a freshman in 1955: Alumni Weekend was one of the best occasions to find a reason to be somewhere else—anywhere else but on campus.

But it wasn't easy to get away, especially if you were in one of the musical groups that would regale the assembled hosts jammed into the events slated for the occasion. Or perhaps you would be part of the student vs. alumni basketball game, where your skill at free throws was not nearly so crucial as CPR.

But dealing with the crowds at the overtaxed facilities was not the really scary part. No—it was the genetic terror stalking the halls of academia that was really unnerving. It was as if Jurassic Park had opened up on campus. And who knew which of these fossils might be lethal as they flocked back to their old haunts.

And yet there was one even more unsettling realization that hung in the air. It was the knowledge among both groups—students and alumni—that we shared a common gene pool. To the returning alumni, it appeared as if the campus had been visited by the outbreak of a virulent and dangerous new genetic mutation that possessed the potential of destroying life as it had always been known. And the students—as they observed the progenitor parade of aging minds and flesh—knew that they were begotten of the same material, which doomed them to similar futures.

And now it was my turn. 1995. Forty years since I arrived as a freshman. I was back on the campus for Alumni Weekend. Then, being possessed by philosophical reflection, it became obvious to me how much we need each other. To reject either our past or our future condemns us to live in a confining present. Without a past, there is no way to project a future. And without a future, the present is meaningless.

The prophet Joel almost seems to be talking about Alumni Weekend when he states that our sons and daughters will "prophecy and see visions" of the future, while those who walked these halls of learning in former years will bring to the mix their "dreams," born of years of experience. And then together we will witness a heavenly presence in which we live together happily ever after.

It shall come to pass afterward, that I will pour out my spirit upon all flesh; and your sons and your daughters shall prophesy, your old men shall dream dreams, your young men shall see visions. Joel 2:28

Gary Patterson is general field secretary of the General Conference of Seventh-day Adventists in Silver Spring, Maryland. He graduated from Walla Walla College in 1959.

SAVED BY A
CLASS ASSIGNMENT *by Robert Johnston*

O ne of my besetting sins in college was procrastination, so I did not welcome the assignment our respected teacher gave us in my advanced Greek class at Pacific Union College. We were to write an essay on our personal understanding of "righteousness by faith."

I couldn't get a handle on it, because the more I thought about it, I discovered I didn't even understand what faith is. I took an Incomplete grade in the course.

Instead of going home for Christmas vacation, I sat alone in my room on the third floor of Newton Hall, strangely exercised over this assignment I had to complete to finish the class. Outside my window was a crystalline night with stars everywhere. An unusual feeling told me that something important was going to happen.

Using a concordance, I began very mechanically to look up Bible texts about faith. Then, using the old one-volume *Index to the Writings of Ellen G. White*, I began looking up her references to the subject. It seemed that each place I read prepared me for the next one. I read: "Feeling is not faith; the two are distinct. Faith is ours to exercise, but joyful feeling and the blessing are God's to give" (*Early Writings*, 72). That helped me.

I turned to the chapter on "Faith and Acceptance" in *Steps to Christ* and began reading. The first two paragraphs hit me between the eyes, for they described my condition perfectly. I had felt out of sync with the whole universe. Then something told me that if I followed the next paragraph like a recipe, something wonderful would happen. So I did.

I read each sentence and did not go on to the next until I had done what it said.

"You have confessed your sins, and in heart put them away." I hadn't, but I did then.

"You have resolved to give yourself to God." I did then.

"Now go to Him, and ask that He will wash away your sins and give you a new heart." I did that too, but I didn't *feel* any different.

"Then believe that He does this *because He has promised*." That's when it happened. A strangely warm feeling filled me, and I've never been the same since.

If we confess our sins, he is faithful and just to forgive us our sins, and to cleanse us from all unrighteousness. 1 John 1:9

Robert Johnston is professor of New Testament and Christian origins at the Seventh-day Adventist Theological Seminary at Andrews University in Berrien Springs, Michigan. He graduated from Pacific Union College in 1953.

HIS GRACE IS SUFFICIENT *By Floyd Greenleaf*

Earning money for my college education was hard. Someone suggested that selling books during the summer was lucrative, so I decided to try it with a couple of friends, Lynn and Nat.

We settled in Wallace, North Carolina, a sleepy hamlet in the tidewater area, surrounded by tobacco fields. My girlfriend's name was Wallace. We had said goodbye a few days earlier in Chattanooga when she returned home to Florida. *Wallace, North Carolina*, I thought. *What a reminder of her.*

Lynn, Nat, and I worked every road in that town. Every night, we marked a map to show where we had been. And three or four nights a week, I wrote a letter from Wallace, North Carolina, to Betty Wallace in West Palm Beach.

June. July. August. Lynn, Nat, and I finally finished selling and decided to vacation a couple weeks before delivering the books and returning to Collegedale. I penciled my last road on the map, packed my suitcase, and headed for Florida, relaxation, sun and sand, Cypress Gardens. And Betty Wallace in Florida was better than Wallace, North Carolina.

All too soon, I returned to work. Deliveries started slowly. I was hot and tired when I returned to my room midafternoon on Friday. The landlady met me at the door. "They's alookin' fer you. A girl's been kilt in Floridy. Car wreck. You 'n' one other the onliest ones in Wallace thet's from Floridy. You bes' git over 'n' find out."

I was stunned. *Only last week, Lord, we laughed together. We talked about our lives. Now she's dead? Please, Lord, I need help.*

That half-mile walk to the telephone office was a struggle to come to grips with the uncertainty of life on this earth. That harsh truth was excruciating for this nineteen-year-old. My heart said life had no more meaning. My head said that life must go on. The Lord said, "My grace is sufficient for you." I believed Him.

I was at peace when I approached the man sitting in the office doorway spitting watermelon seeds. "Everthang's fine. We done delivered the message. Hit ain't fer you."

"Thank you." I could say no more and turned away. "Thank You, Lord. You knew what I did not, but I believed that Your grace was sufficient. Never let me forget the trust You taught me while we walked that half-mile together."

He said unto me, My grace is sufficient for thee. 2 Corinthians 12:9

Floyd Greenleaf is vice president for academic administration of Southern College of Seventh-day Adventists in Collegedale, Tennessee. He graduated from Southern College in 1955.

A VOICE BEHIND   *By Nancy Jean Weber Vyhmeister*

"Please come to the dean's office as soon as you can," read the message. I was baffled. I had done nothing to deserve a reprimand from the dean; my bill was paid, and I was getting good grades.

I was cruising through my junior year at Pacific Union College, dreaming of the interpreter's course I would take in Europe as soon as I finished my degree. With my knowledge of several languages, I would find jobs plentiful—and exciting!

"Miss Weber," the dean announced rather formally, "we need you to teach French next quarter."

I gasped. Of course, I knew that the professor was recovering from a heart attack and could not teach. But that did not mean I should teach. I'd vowed never to be a teacher.

"Of course, the college would pay you," the dean went on, giving a sum that opened my ears.

Quickly calculating the financial benefits and basking in faculty approval, I agreed to teach the class, starting the following week. Outside of the dean's office, I pinched myself. What had I agreed to?

With great trepidation, I met my first class appointment. Of the ten students, several were my friends. How would I manage to teach my peers? I kept reminding myself that *I* knew French; they did not. Also, I was sure that God had a hand in this, as He had in so many other aspects of my life. Nevertheless, I returned to my room after that first class, emotionally drained and physically drenched.

By the end of the first week, I was enjoying myself. The students seemed to be having fun. We were all learning.

By the end of the second week, I made an appointment with the chairman of the education department. To open our conversation, I made the announcement: "I have decided I want to teach." To say that Dr. Normington was surprised would be an understatement. However, he helped me map out a schedule that would allow me to have provisional certification by the time I graduated.

That happened in 1957. Nearly forty years later, I can affirm that I have never regretted paying attention to the voice behind me saying, "This is the way; walk in it."

Whether you turn to the right or to the left, your ears will hear a voice behind you, saying, "This is the way; walk in it." Isaiah 30:21, NIV

Nancy Jean Weber Vyhmeister is professor of mission at the Seventh-day Adventist Theological Seminary at Andrews University in Berrien Springs, Michigan. She graduated from Pacific Union College in 1958.

A REALIZATION
AND A RESOLUTION *By Lon Gruesbeck*

When I enrolled at Pacific Union College in the fall of 1967, I had no idea what I wanted to do with my life. With no clear direction, my ambivalence and my sometimes rebellious attitude became controlling factors in how I related to other people and whether I approved of them.

Perhaps they owned a really "tough" car, and I didn't. Maybe their mannerisms seemed "stuck-up." Whatever the case, I had quickly "pegged" several people on campus, and I wanted nothing to do with them. Did I really know them? No! Yet I was quick to judge them unfit for my association. At the close of my junior year, however, I had a simple wake-up experience that has changed how I see others.

Several of us were in Tom's room down the hall. I disliked Tom for no reason I could identify; I just didn't like him. We were all hanging around joking when I realized, to my great and sheepish surprise, that Tom was really a pretty decent guy to be around. I just hadn't given him the time or the chance to help me see that before.

At that moment of realization, I determined not to pass judgment on others before they had a chance to "show themselves approved." After all, didn't I expect others to give me a fair shake in life? I realized that most people are basically decent, so I must allow myself the opportunity to see their good qualities.

Since that great resolution, have I batted one thousand? No way! Twenty-five years later I still, sometimes, am quick to judge. Often, when I realize what I've done, I'm able to back up and give the individual time and space to prove me wrong. And I've gained some great friendships by not "writing people off" before getting to know them better.

Passing quick judgment is easy to do. Being fair and treating others as I want to be treated requires conscious effort on my part. The dividends are worth the effort. That simple moment of inspiration in a dorm room long ago changed an important part of my life for good.

You judge by human standards; I pass judgment on no one. John 8:15, NIV

Lon Gruesbeck is superintendent of schools of the Chesapeake Conference of Seventh-day Adventists in Columbia, Maryland. He graduated from Pacific Union College in 1971.

THINGS ARE NOT ALWAYS WHAT THEY SEEM *By Paul Kilgore*

The first year of our marriage, while I was attending Southern Missionary College, my wife and I lived in a very small house on campus, so small that it was one of several called "the cracker boxes."

One Sabbath morning, as we were getting ready to attend church in the tabernacle, I heard a knock on the front door of our little house. I opened the door, and there stood a bum. In fairness, that's the only way I can describe him. Ragged clothes, disheveled, dirty. He looked straight at me and said, "I'm hungry. Can you give me something to eat?"

Many things went through my mind. My wife and I were struggling newlyweds, having a hard time keeping enough food on the shelf to feed ourselves. *This bum who won't work is asking me for some of my hard-earned food.* I quickly said, "No," and shut the door in his face.

My wife called out, "Who was that at the door?" I told her it was just a bum wanting something to eat. To my amazement, she asked, "Why didn't you give him something?"

Indignantly I said, "No! We have hardly enough to feed ourselves."

My wife had been brought up with the idea that as long as you have something on your shelves, you should share. She asked me to go find the man while she found something for him to eat.

I went to the front door, expecting to see him close by. He was nowhere to be found. Hardly more than a minute had passed between my "No" and the commencement of my search. I got in the car and drove up and down the road. No bum. We asked our friends if they had seen such a man that morning. No one had.

Of course, I can't prove to anyone that God was specifically testing me that morning. I don't know positively that He sent one of His angels to see if I would be willing to care for someone less fortunate. But I have been haunted by that thought from that day until now.

I do believe that the Lord sent an angel that morning to test my Christianity and give my good wife a chance to teach me that I can always share something.

Do not forget to entertain strangers, for by doing so, some people have entertained angels without knowing it. Hebrews 13:2, NEV

Paul Kilgore is director of education of the Atlantic Union Conference of Seventh-day Adventists in South Lancaster, Massachusetts. He graduated from Southern College in 1957.

PACO'S INCREDIBLE WEEK *By Frank Ottati*

As a young man, Paco believed he was called by the Lord to be a minister. He applied to attend the Seventh-day Adventist college in Lima, Peru, to study theology.

When he arrived at the school, he assumed that all the students there who were studying to be pastors were probably "saints." The reality was somewhat disappointing, but Paco was not discouraged. He studied hard, although occasionally he had grave doubts about his calling to the ministry. "Is God really calling me?" he asked. "Or is it just my imagination?"

One day, while sitting by the basketball court, he prayed, asking the Lord for a sign to "confirm" his call. Paco knew that the only way he could earn his tuition for the next school year was by selling Adventist books during the summer. So he bargained with the Lord. "If You really want me to be a minister," he prayed, "then I will be able to sell enough books to earn a scholarship for next school year."

To earn a scholarship, he needed to sell and deliver fifty collections of books. While he had the Lord's attention, Paco pushed a little further. "And if You really are calling me into the ministry," he prayed, "You will answer my prayer in the first two weeks of work."

That summer, ninety students from the Adventist college went out to canvass in different cities throughout Peru. Paco and a friend were assigned to the city of Huacho. They had no friends there, only a small Adventist church.

The first week, Paco sold nothing. On Monday of the second week, he sold fifteen collections. Tuesday, he sold ten sets. On Wednesday, he sold twelve; on Thursday, eleven; and on Friday, six. In five days, Paco had sold fifty-four book collections. Of the fifty-four sets, he delivered and received payment for fifty-three. The Lord had answered his prayer. "Yes, yes," He seemed to reply. "You will be a minister for Me."

This is a very personal story. In Spanish, Paco is the nickname for Frank, and I am that Paco. I can never doubt that the Lord has called me into the gospel ministry to bring many people to the foot of the cross. And I can never doubt that God answers my prayers.

Ask and it will be given to you; seek and you will find; knock and the door will be opened to you. For everyone who asks receives; he who seeks finds; and to him who knocks, the door will be opened. Matthew 7:7, 8, NIV

Frank Ottati is ministerial director of the Columbia Union Conference of Seventh-day Adventists in Columbia, Maryland. He graduated from Inca Union University in 1967.

THE APPLE OF HIS EYE *By Don Corkum*

My self-concept was changed one evening while I was a student at Atlantic Union College.

I had attended public school through tenth grade, so I missed much of what Christian education provides in leadership development and music training. Most students at the college had talents and abilities that I didn't possess. I wanted to be a minister but was unsure of what contribution I could make to the church. Was I valuable and important to God?

On Friday evenings, Paul Riley, the men's dean, usually took a group of dorm students somewhere for prayer bands after evening vespers. On this Friday evening, he suggested that we walk up Kilbourne Hill, spread out, and pray individually. It was a beautiful evening. The stars stood out brightly. I had just taken an astronomy course and was keenly aware of the vast, incomprehensible size of the universe.

At first, I started a vigorous dialogue with God about how I was really nobody in such a big universe. I was like a speck of cosmic dust in His vast creation. How could I possibly be valuable to Him?

After about fifteen minutes of this, something happened. It seemed as if God spoke to me. He told me, as it were, to look down around me. I became aware of the sounds of traffic around South Lancaster and the glow of light in the sky from the town of Clinton beyond. God said, "These are the people I need you to reach for Me. You have a place that no one else can fill. Remember I will always be with you."

That night's silent conversation with God on top of Kilbourne Hill has been an anchor point in my life. I recognize that although there are billions of others in this world, God has a special place for me that no one else can fill. I am *important* to God.

He who touches you touches the apple of his eye. Zechariah 2:8, RSV

Don Corkum is president of the Alberta Conference of Seventh-day Adventists in Red Deer, Alberta. He graduated from Atlantic Union College in 1965.

GENTLE SOUL SCULPTORS *By Morian Perry*

"His gentle means of sculpting souls took me years to understand" (from the song "The Leader of the Band," by Dan Fogelberg).

My father rests on an open knoll in the Washelli Cemetery with trees and Seattle skyscrapers as a backdrop. During the years I attended Walla Walla College, I spent the summers trimming hedges at this place. There was so much to do that when I finished the round, the plants were ready for another shearing.

I had passed this spot hundreds of times. How could I have known that someday my father would rest here? His tombstone is simply marked:

Michael James Perry
Born: April 8, 1911
Died: September 10, 1991
"All That Thrills My Soul Is Jesus"

In the song quoted above, Dan Fogelberg came to appreciate the firm but gentle manner of his talented musician father. Unlike his father, mine wasn't musical. But he would occasionally pick up a little old accordion or sit down at the organ and stumble through a song that he would play by ear. It was always the same—"All That Thrills My Soul Is Jesus."

Several times during those college years, I received desperate calls from my mother summoning me home because Dad was in serious shape and "might not make it through the night." Each medical crisis made me more calloused. Was it really this serious, or was it just Mother being overly concerned?

Only since my father's death have I fully appreciated the man he really was. Nobody can replace his humor, his creativity and his gentle soul sculpting, even though I would not have admitted it then. There were times, of course, when I felt it was far from gentle.

Looking back, I am beginning to realize that a number of other gentle soul sculptors have participated in the sculpting of my cold clay: my mother, my teachers, camp counselors, pastors, and friends. Even more important has been that Master Craftsman, who has guided the hands of these human artisans in their work.

His gentle way of sculpting souls took me years to understand.

God is educating you; that's why you must never drop out. He's treating you as dear children. This trouble you're in isn't punishment; it's *training*, the normal experience of children. Only irresponsible parents leave children to fend for themselves. Would you prefer an irresponsible God? . . . God is doing what is best for us, training us to live God's holy best." The Message, Hebrews 12:10, 11

Morian Perry is superintendent of schools of the Idaho Conference of Seventh-day Adventists in Boise, Idaho. He graduated from Walla Walla College in 1961.

GOD'S GRADUATION GIFT *By Antonio Bueno*

Most college students defer marriage plans until graduation. I didn't. Having found the girl of my dreams, I decided that college life would be much more enjoyable if spent in close association with my lovely Liliane. Fortunately, she concurred, and one August afternoon we were married.

As a theology major, I took a number of interesting courses in Old and New Testament, Church History, Homiletics, etc., which I enjoyed immensely. My teachers, a team of learned and dedicated Christians, patiently endeavored to impress my searching mind with truth from God's Word. They helped me gain a great deal of knowledge about several fascinating theological concepts, such as the tender love of God the Father toward His children and the precious gift of Christ, His Son, for us.

All that was great, but somehow I felt there was a dimension missing in my theological training. I needed something on the experiential level that would help me better understand God's love.

During my senior year, the quarters went by at an ever-increasing speed. Graduation was just around the corner! There would be great joy, family celebration, and numerous gifts from friends and relatives—some more valuable than others.

But the most precious and meaningful gift of all arrived from God, via my beloved wife, just in time for graduation. It was a living gift that looked so much like me. It ate voraciously like me, it slept soundly like me, it even smiled and frowned like me! It was my first child. My son. A being so dear to me that I wouldn't give him up for anything in the world. Someone I immediately loved in a way I had never loved anyone before, for I loved him as a father. Rather, as his father.

And now, it all made sense. All my perplexing theological cogitations about God's fatherly love suddenly came into focus. I realized that in the past I had only had a partial perception of the Father's love, a perception from the receiving end. But now I understood the love of a father from the giving end. Ever since birth, I had known what it was to be loved by a father. Now I grasped the meaning of loving as a father, and I could relate to the Father in a new, more complete way.

But what really filled my mind with indescribable awe was to realize the surpassing greatness of the Father's love for me. For even though He loved His only begotten Son at least as much as I loved mine, God gave Jesus for me! Something that I as a father wouldn't dream of doing even for my best friend, let alone for an enemy, God did for me (see Romans 5:6-11). Amazing love, indeed!

As I tenderly held my tiny son close to my chest on that sunny commencement morning, I thanked the Father for teaching me a most valuable lesson about Himself through His graduation gift.

For God so loved the world, that he gave his only begotten Son, that

**whosoever believeth in him should not perish, but have everlasting
life. John 3:16**

*Antonio Bueno is assistant professor of theology at the Seventh-day Adventist Theological Seminary
at Andrews University. He graduated from Saleve Adventist Institute in 1977.*

I WANTED TO QUIT   *By LouAnn Howard*

For as long as I could remember, I wanted to teach elementary school. I
never seriously considered another line of work, even when the aptitude test I took during my senior year of academy indicated a stronger
interest in other fields. So I began my college education as an elementary-
education major and loved it.

During my junior year, something went wrong. My grades were still
good. My job in the library was still challenging and interesting. My friends
were still friends. But something was missing. I no longer had the desire to
study, to learn, to remain in school. It seemed as though my world had
stopped, and I was getting nowhere on an endless treadmill. The thought
of enduring another year was depressing. I wanted to be through with
college and begin my career.

Quitting was a viable option. I had the skills necessary to get a secretarial
job in the community, and I knew I would excel at that position. Secretarial
work was interesting to me. I had worked in many such jobs and had enjoyed each one of them. However, that didn't seem right for me either.

My parents recognized that I was in conflict. We talked about what was
troubling me, but they didn't really know what advice to give me. Because
I lived at home, we had plenty of opportunity to discuss the options, but
no clear solution ever came.

What turned things around? Nothing, in any dramatic way. I simply stuck
with my studies and other activities. Gradually the feeling of frustration
left. I believe I got over my confusion because I depended on the Lord to
guide. I determined not to change my focus unless I received a clearer
directive than just a vague restlessness. After my junior year, I never had
another doubt that the Lord was calling me to teach. I thoroughly enjoyed
my senior year and am grateful for the way the Lord led me through my
time of discouragement.

I learned that God is always there, even when I am unsure, confused,
discouraged, or bored. He will lead me through the difficult times.

You are my rock and my fortress; therefore, for Your name's sake, lead

me and guide me. Psalm 31:3, NKJV

LouAnn Howard is superintendent of schools of the Illinois Conference of Seventh-day Adventists in Brookfield, Illinois. She graduated from Union College in 1978.

WELCOME BACK! By J. Wayne Coulter

I entered the gymnasium tentatively, even sheepishly, and crossed the floor to the assigned table. Several years had passed since I had last registered for classes at Southern College. The reason for my absence brought embarrassment every time I thought about it. And now, here I was, trying again, as a freshman, hoping people had forgotten.

"Wayne Coulter!" I immediately recognized the voice of Dr. Everett Watrous. "Welcome back! It's so good to see you again." His friendliness immediately put me at ease, and I began to hope.

Contacts with faculty in the days ahead proved, to my amazement, how they apparently had forgotten what I so shamefully remembered. I had been a freshman. Some older students had stolen some tools and materials from the college garage. I hadn't been involved in the theft, but I had helped them hide the stolen property. Some time later, one of the fellows tried to sell a stolen battery in town, and our crime was uncovered.

The administration, quite rightly, ordered some serious discipline if we were to remain at the college. Dr. Kenneth Wright, the president, pleaded with me to stick it out, accept the discipline, and prove myself. He shared a text with me—Philippians 4:13: "I can do all things through Jesus Christ who strengthens me" (NKJV).

Unfortunately, I ignored his pleadings. I couldn't bear the thought that everybody in that community would look at me as a thief. So I left college. And I left the church. But I never forgot my conversation with Dr. Wright.

Now, several years later, I was back. I found warmth and acceptance. And I spent the next four years at Southern College preparing for a place in

God's work. Who ever would have thought I would make it? But soon, with those years of preparation, I was ready to face the world. My confidence in Scripture and Christ was confirmed. Surely *we* can do *anything* through Christ!

I can do all things through Christ who strengthens me. Philippians 4:13, NKJV

J. Wayne Coulter is president of the Illinois Conference of Seventh-day Adventists in Brookfield, Illinois. He graduated from Southern College in 1966.

THE YOUNG MISCREANTS *By Larry Provonsha*

As I look back on my college years, two groups of students stand out: those who always seemed to be in trouble and those who were model students. The model students were, of course, not completely perfect. They complained occasionally about required worships and were late to their classes. Some were even known to play Rook in the dormitory!

But to my group of friends and me, it seemed that the rascals had honed misbehavior to a fine and delicate art. Chapel, with its captive audience, was a favorite venue for pranks. One elaborate scheme, which sent students screaming in every direction, involved a number of laboratory mice attached to tiny parachutes descending from openings in the blue coffered ceiling of old Irwin Hall. Another chapel service was disrupted when several dozen alarm clocks secured under chairs rang in unison.

One of the most notorious and long-lasting behaviors that caused much head shaking among the Angwin saints occurred frequently during Sabbath-morning worship services. Some village students, in their modified cars, would meet for drag racing. They revved up their unmuffled engines and accelerated down the quarter-mile stretch adjacent to the church. Sometimes the minister would pause until the roar of racing hot rods faded into the distance.

I understand that more recent years have witnessed little decline in pranks. But the years since my college graduation have taught me that all is not always as it appears. Far too many of my meticulously rule-keeping classmates have left the church to pursue success in the world's eyes.

And what of the young miscreants who tortured the faculty and administration so creatively? Many of them are deacons and elders, ministers and church-school teachers. Their articles appear in the *Review* and other church publications. They are conference presidents and union conference officials. They are dedicated and true Christians of many professions working for the Lord.

I picture the pews of our churches—and someday the courts of heaven—filled with reformed rascals whom the Lord saw as precious jewels waiting to be polished.

The Lord seeth not as man seeth; for man looketh on the outward appearance, but the Lord looketh on the heart. 1 Samuel 16:7

Larry Provonsha is an investigation specialist for the state of California in Sacramento and vice chairman of the board of Pacific Union College. He graduated from Pacific Union College in 1966.

RUN TO WIN *By Jim Clizbe*

As a college student, I loved all team sports. On the field or court, however, my performance rarely matched my passion. I hardly ever made it on an A-league team.

My uncertainty about my athletic ability or, rather, a frank estimation of it caused me much anxiety in college. After all, I was a physical education major. I had reason to worry that my career choice of PE teaching wasn't logical. Most PE majors at Andrews University were "jocks" or superstars. I was only a B-league player.

A conference with the department chair, Ingrid Johnson, helped put things in proper perspective. Miss Johnson would not have been classified as a superstar in athletics either, but she was a very caring and encouraging teacher. She stressed the importance of doing my best in each of the sports. But she also taught me that knowing how to help or teach a struggling student to learn the basic skills of the game was much more important than winning at any cost or being a superstar myself.

Miss Johnson's philosophy and powerful example contributed to a wholesome attitude toward competition and sportsmanship among her students. The support and influence of this caring and sincere teacher continue to have a ripple effect in elementary and secondary schools today. The many of her students who are teachers or administrators are continuing to encourage the wishful superstars.

You know that in a race all the runners run. But only one gets the prize. So run like that. Run to win! 1 Corinthians 9:24, The Youth Bible

Jim Clizbe is superintendent of schools of the Southern California Conference of Seventh-day Adventists in Glendale, California. He graduated from Andrews University in 1965.

BLOND HAIR AND TRUST *By Orville Parchment*

The day was bright and sunny. I was excited as I climbed into the cockpit of the Cessna 150 to continue my flight instruction at Andrews University. The instructor said that it was time for my first lesson in instrument flying.

After taking off and climbing to a few thousand feet, I was handed a hood to put over my head. This prevented me from seeing anything but the instrument panel while I flew the plane.

When the lesson was over, I returned to my Garland apartment on the Andrews campus. I hurried in to share with Jean, my bride of only eight months, the excitement of my first instrument lesson. After I was through explaining the details, she calmly asked, "Where did you get those strands of blond hair on your sweater?"

Sure enough, there they were. I was just as puzzled as Jean about the origin of those strands. I simply said, "That's a mystery." I knew that I hadn't been in close-enough proximity to anyone with long blond hair to have it show up on my sweater. Jean's hair was very dark brown. We said nothing more about the little mystery.

The following week, I went again for my lesson in instrument flying. Once again, I had to put on the hood. As I did, I saw strands of blond hair tangled in the swivels on either side of the hood. The student who had her lesson before me had blond hair, and she also was taking instrument flying. Some of her hair got caught in the hood and then stuck to my sweater when it was my turn to use the hood.

The mystery of the blond hair was never a concern to Jean or me, but it was still very puzzling. We both smiled as I explained to her how it had happened.

I am thankful that the love that God has placed in our hearts for each other has caused us to trust each other completely and have peace in our hearts even when the evidence raises questions.

The peace of God, which transcends all understanding, will guard your hearts and your minds in Christ Jesus. Philippians 4:7, NIV

Orville Parchment is president of the Seventh-day Adventist Church in Canada in Oshawa, Ontario, and chairman of the board of Canadian Union College. He graduated from Andrews University in 1973.

COLLEGE JUNIOR
MEETS SENIOR ANGEL *By D. Ronald Watts*

Early in September, 1956 I completed my Christian book sales and began a 2,200-mile drive from Ontario to Canadian Union College in Alberta for my junior year. The first day's drive brought me to Emmanuel Missionary College (Andrews University) in Michigan, where I spent the night. Wide awake with excitement the second night, I didn't stop at all.

The third evening, after thirty-six straight hours at the wheel, I took a sunset timeout to view "Old Faithful" in Yellowstone. As darkness fell, I began navigating the precipitous hairpin highway that descends from Yellowstone's north entrance. Drowsiness came with the darkness, and I felt a great need to close my eyes. But there was no place to pull over. Anyway, there was no way I could fall asleep with all those twists and turns to keep me alert.

I was wrong. A sudden violence shook the car as it left the road and crossed the ditch. My head hit the door on the driver's side of the car. Instantly, I was wide awake. That same second, I saw in the beam of the headlights that I was sailing through open space headed for destruction on great rocks below. I cried out, "Lord, save me!"

Instantly, the car changed direction in midair and gently settled back on the highway in the smoothest landing I have ever experienced. I was even in the right lane! I stopped the car and thought, *Did this really happen, or have I been dreaming?* I tried to open the door, but the chrome strip from the front fender was twisted back against the door, and it would not open. The passenger door was in the same condition. The Christian tracts from the back window were under the brake pedal. It was not a dream.

The angel of the Lord encamps around those who fear him, and he delivers them. Psalm 34:7, NIV

D. Ronald Watts is president of the British Columbia Conference of Seventh-day Adventists in Abbotsford, British Columbia. He graduated from Canadian Union College in 1958.

HELPFUL EMBARRASSMENT *By Calvin B. Rock*

I didn't know how it would end, but after three years of financial struggle, barely staying ahead of the dreaded order to drop all classes—the notice came! I was in the middle of my sophomore year. I had no money to stay in school, no money to go home, and no alternative but to work full time while my classmates proceeded with their studies and exams.

Being put out of school because of an unpaid bill was far from unheard of. But I had worked on the farm and in maintenance and had really hoped to avoid the inconvenience and yes, the embarrassment.

But there I was on the roof of the latest campus building project, pounding nails, watching and sometimes waving to my friends who were going to class. The roof was high; the weather was cold; my spirits were low. I thought it all so unfair—not the school's rules but the fate that I was suffering. I had gone as far as I could, and there seemed to be no way out of my constant battle to make it financially.

How did it all come out? Well, my praying, sacrificing mother sent more funds, and a member of the church back home anonymously contributed a sizable sum as well. After a few weeks, I was allowed to return to class, make up the lost work, and finish the school year. That was not the last financial crisis I faced while a student at Oakwood College, but it truly was the last time I feared the outcome.

Twenty-one years after that hard experience in my sophomore year, I returned to Oakwood College as its eighth president. During my tenure, students often benefited from very liberal (some people would say *too* liberal) student-aid policies.

What they and the faculty didn't know was that each time I was forced to weigh action regarding a financially strapped student, I was moved to be as helpful as possible by the memory of my own struggles in similar circumstances.

Now, many years later, I still regard my dismissal from classes as a very difficult time. But I am most gratified by the successes of so many students who stayed in school because of policies informed by that experience.

My greatest hope is that as I was privileged to be helpful to them, they will in turn keep the dynamics flowing by helping others.

Praise be to the God and Father of our Lord Jesus Christ, the Father of compassion and the God of all comfort, who comforts us in all our troubles, so that we can comfort those in any trouble with the comfort we ourselves have received from God. 2 Corinthians 1:3, 4, NIV

Calvin B. Rock is general vice president of the General Conference of Seventh-day Adventists in Silver Spring, Maryland, and chairman of the board of Loma Linda University. He graduated from Oakwood College in 1954.

IN THE DRIVER'S SEAT   *By Melvin K. Eisele*

At the end of my sophomore year at Union College, I prepared to work as a student literature evangelist for the summer in northern Iowa. I had gotten very little sleep the last several nights before beginning the 250-mile trip to the summer training school. When I finally headed out at about 6:00 on a Sunday evening, I was very tired. I drove for several hours on two-lane roads. Anxiously, I counted the miles, constantly calculating my time of arrival.

The last road sign I remember seeing indicated I was still forty miles from Des Moines. I estimated I had another hour of driving.

The loud blast of a trucker's air horn was the next thing that caught my attention. I sat up in the seat just enough to see the bright truck lights and wonder what all the fuss was about. I was very tired, and I needed more rest, I said to myself. So carefully I laid back down on the seat and noticed just then that a bridge passed by overhead.

Something within me told me I must be passing under the road I should take north for the last thirty miles to where the training school would begin in a few hours. But that is all I thought—just that I should be on that road.

When I awoke again, I was still lying down on the front seat of the car. Now I could see street lights flashing by as the car passed under them. It puzzled me to see these street lights. I hadn't planned to drive through any large city.

Suddenly, I came to my senses, sat up in a great fright, and looked around. *I was in the driver's seat behind the steering wheel!* I grabbed it and stopped the car. Then I began searching for the driver. Perhaps I had picked up a hitchhiker, I thought in my confusion. Or maybe I had taken along a passenger and had forgotten about who had been doing the driving. There was not a trace of anyone in or around the car.

I turned the car around and began driving. Seven miles later—seven miles of curvy, two-lane road—I came to the bridge and the road north.

I was convicted then, and still am today, that my angel had driven the car. We serve a tender, compassionate God.

The angel of the Lord encamps around those who fear him, and he delivers them. Taste and see that the Lord is good; blessed is the man who takes refuge in him. Psalms 34:7, 8, NIV

Melvin K. Eisele is treasurer of the Gulf States Conference of Seventh-day Adventists in Montgomery, Alabama. He graduated from Union College in 1971.

YOU'RE STUDYING WHAT?! *By Phyllis Ware*

Ralph and I have been best friends since we met during our freshman year at the University of Notre Dame.

I was from Kansas City, Missouri; a Catholic since age six; and had attended Catholic schools from elementary through high school. Although I was a good student, the small schools I attended left me feeling out of place on this big university campus. My mother died the summer after my freshman year, and I struggled to maintain even a marginal interest in my classes.

Ralph had been a straight-"A" student throughout high school in Phenix City, Alabama, but he struggled with the strenuous academics at Notre Dame. After a difficult freshman year, he changed majors from electrical engineering to business administration. That put us on the same academic track.

We were close friends, spending many days together studying, hanging out in the student union, frequenting the snack bar, or riding our bikes into town.

One evening, we made plans for some last-minute study together before a Principles of Accounting exam. Ralph never showed up, so I left the Breen-Phillips dorm, where I lived, and headed in the direction of the exam. Suddenly Ralph came running, "What happened to you?" I asked. "I forgot I had Bible-study class," he responded. "Bible study!!" I yelled incredulously. "You?!"

As I now review my reaction, I understand why Ralph kept secret his weekly Bible-study classes with two Andrews University seminarians. Several weeks before, he had responded to a self-addressed stamped post card slipped under his door asking if he had a Bible question to be answered. Neither Ralph nor I ever conceived that the other had any real interest in religion.

Once the secret was out, I also began studying with the Adventists, and that summer at the age of twenty, I was baptized into the Linwood Boulevard Seventh-day Adventist Church in Kansas City, Missouri. Ralph was baptized the following summer.

Ralph now has a wife and four children, and two of his daughters attend Southern College in Collegedale, Tennessee.

I have learned not to be discouraged when people seem indifferent or unconcerned about spiritual matters. God knew that two apparently indifferent college students at Notre Dame were searching for something better than this world had to offer. He sent two seminary students from Andrews to sow the seed of truth at Notre Dame. I am thankful for His patience.

Blessed are ye that sow beside all waters, that send forth thither the feet of the ox and the ass. Isaiah 32:20

Phyllis Ware is secretary-treasurer of the Central States Conference of Seventh-day Adventists in Kansas City, Kansas. She graduated from the University of Notre Dame in 1977.

STUDYING IS HOLY *By Jacques Doukhan*

I am overwhelmed—suffocated by studying again; reviewing all this vast, arcane, and boring material I have gathered during the quarter. Am I not wasting my time with all this irrelevant information?

Certainly, God would rather see me involved only in holy and spiritual activities. I feel so frustrated and helpless, and my mind revolts against this base enterprise of studying.

Suddenly, I am struck by an astounding irony and a passionate appeal: studying, indeed, is holy. And this is so not just when I study the Bible, invigorating my mind with holy stories about God's righteousness and love. Rather, studying is holy per se, in and of itself.

I learned that lesson slowly and painfully during college.

Studying is holy, because it draws me out of myself. It forces me to listen to someone else and to be exposed to new and different truths. Thus, it helps develop my ability to listen to the other person, to see, and to love my neighbor.

Studying is holy, because it sharpens my power of concentration on the essential, the invisible, and eventually improves my capacity to pray, to meditate and have faith.

Studying is holy, because it forces me to calm down and pause, to experience silence in the noisy turmoil of my daily life.

But above all, *studying is holy*, because it is a humbling experience; it confronts me with the infinite and makes me aware of my limitations and needs.

This lesson hides itself, powerful and unexpected, on the hard path of any studying experience. God is there when we study math, history, literature, philosophy, languages, just as He is there when we open our Bible. When we study, we fulfill God's purpose.

When we understand this strange lesson, our college life makes sense in His hands. Then silence, deep thinking, right thinking, and carefulness invade our lives, to help make them, right now, masterpieces.

When studying is holy, then life is holier.

Much study is wearisome to the flesh. Ecclesiastes 12:12, NKJV

Jacques Doukhan is professor of Hebrew and Old Testament exegesis at Andrews University in Berrien Springs, Michigan. He graduated from the University of Strasbourg in 1970.

A MIND-BLOWING PROFESSOR *By Dan Smith*

I came to college as an eighteen-year-old, straight from the mission field with my package of beliefs. Every Wednesday, one of my college professors would blow my mind.

There were only six of us in his class—bright, free-thinking guys. He would point out what seemed to be minor inconsistencies among the Gospels. For instance, the same events were told in different order. I couldn't believe this. How could a God of truth inspire writers to write things down in the wrong order? My first reaction was to question why the college allowed this heretic to teach here. Every Wednesday night at ten o'clock, I would trudge back to my room with my naive faith shattered. If there were minor mistakes, how could I trust the rest of the Bible?

The professor refused to give any quick answers. He would let us stew, wrestling to find our own.

Soon I found myself enduring a familiar pattern: my faith would be built up during the week in other classes, only to be smashed again Wednesday night. Gradually, however, I began to form my own theology of inspiration, a theology that held onto the Bible as God's inspired Word. It was a Bible with truth enough to know God and Christ and give me a worldview that made sense and worked for me. But it was also a Bible with some human aspects that God chose not to overrule.

That professor's gift was not obvious to me, nor entirely valued, until years later when the Desmond Ford/Walter Rea inspiration controversies hit. My peers were now having their minds blown. I was fine. I had been prepared years before by a wise teacher who forced me to wrestle with hard questions, to define my own beliefs in a way that could handle the evidence. He helped me establish a faith that I could defend. He has forever since been my favorite college teacher.

Often we discover new evidence that conflicts with our established paradigms, and we wonder if we will ever get back to calm waters of certainty. But the God of Sunday resurrections has always come through for me with a new paradigm, a better, bigger theology, that includes the new evidence. God is still in the business of creating light out of darkness.

The god of this age has blinded the minds of unbelievers, . . . [but] God, who said, "Let light shine out of darkness," made his light shine in our hearts to give us the light of the knowledge of the glory of God in the face of Christ. 2 Corinthians 4:4-6, NIV

Dan Smith is senior pastor of La Sierra University Church in Riverside, California. He graduated from Pacific Union College in 1974.

THE IMMINENT DROPOUT
AND THE ECCENTRIC PROF
By Ralph W. Perrin

The first moment I saw him, I knew he was an eccentric. He wore his hair in a crewcut, seemingly oblivious to the shoulder-length fashion preferred by many of his male students. This tall young professor, with a Ph.D. from Duke University, displayed a passion for biological research that had us new students awestruck. I was intimidated by his penetrating eyes and probing questions that could quickly cause an unprepared student to feel uncomfortable in his presence.

My first impression was that he was unapproachable, aloof, and inaccessible. I judged him to be the last teacher I would ever go to if I needed help.

My ambition since high school was to be a biology teacher. And yet, after two and a half quarters at Walla Walla College, I was ready to drop all of my classes and find a job in a field that didn't require a college degree and was far from my interest of biology. The pressure of trying to make decent grades in a concentrated biology curriculum while working four hours every night in a local sawmill had proved to be too much. No other major than biology would do, and I had to work at least twenty hours a week to help finance my education. The apparent answer was to quit college.

I don't know why Dr. Larry McCloskey invited me into his office that afternoon. He could not have known that I had already filled out a drop slip, for I had told no one. He was a busy man who spent incredibly long hours on class preparation and research. But for two hours it seemed like there was nothing he would rather do than sit and talk with me. I saw those penetrating eyes soften as he talked about his passion for biology, teaching, and research. My perception of his aloofness melted away as I saw him take genuine interest in my goals and concerns. His story about God's leading in his life in many ways paralleled my own.

Leaving his office with encouragement and a new resolve to stay in college, I tore up my drop slip. I am convinced that God used an eccentric professor to help focus a free-spirited college student that spring afternoon. I am forever grateful to Dr. McCloskey for that one office visit that changed my life.

Moses told the people, "Don't be afraid. Just stand where you are and watch, and you will see the wonderful way the Lord will rescue you today." Exodus 14:13, TLB

Ralph W. Perrin is dean for student affairs of Loma Linda University in Loma Linda, California. He graduated from Walla Walla College in 1977.

THE DOORKEEPER *By Charles Bell*

The cargo-size steel doors of the Glendale Power Plant lay in a twisted heap on the dock. With them lay my hopes for earning enough money to continue my engineering studies.

The summer had begun better. I had spotted a notice at the power plant's employment office. They needed a mechanic's assistant. It would be a sweltering job, but twenty Mississippi summers had prepared me for just such conditions. The minimum wage in 1954 was not much, but neither was the tuition for my junior year at Mississippi State. I learned that field engineers from General Electric were overhauling a massive electric generator and its steam turbine. My enthusiasm soared higher when Mr. Carter assigned me to the eighty-ton-capacity traveling crane. I learned fast and soon could adjust the Big Hook within a few thousandths of an inch. But one Friday, Carter announced that we would work on Saturday. I had just left my Southern Baptist tradition to become an Adventist. When I tried to explain, Carter fired me on the spot. I cleaned out my locker and walked off toward the bus stop. Before I got there, Carter apparently changed his mind and bellowed, "Bell! Come back on Monday!"

After that close call, I *didn't* need this new disaster! Carter had asked me to take the crane to the end of the dock near the power plant and unload a large transformer from a railroad flatcar. I responded quickly, grateful for the break from the tedious micro-inch adjustments for the GE engineers. Then, I heard the sickening crunch. The giant doors of the power plant were ripped from their hinges by the world's newest crane operator. Though it was impossible for me to have seen from the crane that the doors were open across the track, I knew that I was in deep trouble. Who would pay for those expensive doors? I inched, cringing, down the long ladder from the crane's cab, preparing to hear Carter's ionizing words, "You're *really* fired!"

But the King had other plans for his new son. There was not one word of condemnation. Instead, Carter roughed up a plant operator, for leaving the doors open. I still suspect that I was more at fault than the operator but I'm grateful that the King of glory came through those torn doors and touched Carter's heart. Someone else took the blame for my offense.

Jesus takes the blame for *all* our offenses.

Lift up your heads, O you gates; be lifted up, you ancient doors, that the King of glory may come in. Psalm 24:7, NIV

Charles Bell is vice president for academic administration of Pacific Union College in Angwin, California. He graduated from Mississippi State University in 1956.

THE ROLLER COASTER
AND THE SIGN *By James J. North, Jr.*

A ll she said was, "If we break up, I'll never see you again!"

• • • • •

One day in May of 1958, I sat on the men's side of Machlan Auditorium at Atlantic Union College. Visiting Adventist public-high-school seniors were introducing themselves. A young woman sitting almost directly across the aisle stood and in her New England accent said, "I am Audrey Jones from Brockton High School in Brockton, Massachusetts." I was impressed.

Four months later, I recognized her immediately during fall registration. Before long, we were dating—and walking on air.

And then I put us on a long roller coaster of confidence and doubt about our relationship. In June, I would break up with her and then barely survive the summer. In the fall, I'd start things up again. Then, later during the school year, I'd trouble her with my doubts about us.

She was taking nursing, and I was in theology. In 1960, when I graduated and headed for seminary at Andrews University, she conveniently enrolled at Hinsdale Sanitarium, not far away in Chicago.

I wasn't sure what to do. I asked the Lord to give me some indication that she was the "right one." I wanted a sign.

We got engaged in September of 1961. One evening, while we were driving from Hinsdale to Andrews, I again began to express doubts about our relationship.

All she said was, "If we break up, I'll never see you again!" I knew that one of her strongest characteristics was honesty. She didn't "play games." But I never expected such a shocking ultimatum, such a "sign." I needed no other.

Actually, there were many "signs," and I should have given them more weight: our devotion to God and ministry; our shared attitudes and views; the way we worked out our differences; our bond of love; the physical attraction we longed to express; our desire for a family. And certainly not the least of these signs was our amazing ability to survive my roller coaster.

Practical premarital counseling from Charles Wittschiebe helped greatly. We were married on August 12, 1962. We've been happily married now for more than three decades. What started so haltingly during those roller-coaster days has lasted all these happy years.

Dating in college will inevitably include times of doubt and the heartbreak of changing relationships. These prepare us for that one special relationship that God blesses with inseparable marriage. Pray constantly for guidance. Watch for the "signs," even shocking ones, like the one I was given. Get premarital counseling. Then join hands and hearts "till death do us part!"

They are no longer two but one flesh. What therefore God has joined together, let not man put asunder. Matthew 19:6, RSV

James J. North, Jr., is associate professor of pastoral care and chaplaincy at the Seventh-day Adventist Theological Seminary at Andrews University in Berrien Springs, Michigan. He graduated from Atlantic Union College in 1960.

A COMMENT AND A CAREER CHANGE By James Nix

School administrators hope Weeks of Prayer will provide life-changing experiences for students. Growing up in the Adventist system, I attended my share. Although today I cannot recall even the names of most of the speakers, one Week of Prayer—in quite an unexpected way—changed my life.

I was attending La Sierra College at the time. During one Week of Prayer meeting, the speaker described an elderly woman who attended the church he pastored. He told how she usually nodded in agreement as he spoke, though occasionally she would shake her head in disagreement. When such happened, he knew he needed to make a pastoral visit!

The woman was Mrs. Alma McKibbin, author of our first Adventist church-school Bible textbooks. Our speaker also commented that this very spry nonagenarian had known many early pioneers, including Elders S. N. Haskell and J. N. Loughborough, as well as Ellen G. White.

For some reason, it had previously never dawned on me that there were people then living who remembered Mrs. White. Our speaker's comments piqued my curiosity. During our next school break, I went to visit Mrs. McKibbin. What a privilege that turned out to be! Soon there were more visits. Ellen White's daughter-in-law, the widow of Elder William C. White, as well as five of Ellen White's seven grandchildren were then living. In addition, others also shared their recollections of Mrs. White and the pioneers.

Quite excited, I added theology to my history major. Previously, I never had thought about becoming a minister. Little could I have known as I entered the seminary at Andrews University that rather than my going into the pastoral ministry, God had other plans for my life.

After graduation, I was invited to Loma Linda University to start Heritage Rooms on both the La Sierra and Loma Linda campuses. In the years that followed, as critics came along attacking Ellen White and her work, I knew much of what they were saying was untrue. Why? Because in addition to her writings, I recalled the personal recollections shared by many, most of whom were deceased by then whose memories of Ellen White did not square with the descriptions of her attackers.

Yes, it was just a simple Week of Prayer illustration. But nearly thirty years later, the results of that comment still play out every day in my work.

Since we are surrounded by such a great cloud of witnesses, let us throw off everything that hinders and the sin that so easily entangles, and let us run with perseverance the race marked out for us. Hebrews 12:1, NIV

James Nix is vice director of the Ellen G. White Estate at the General Conference of Seventh-day Adventists in Silver Spring, Maryland. He graduated from La Sierra University in 1969.

WEATHERING A TIDAL WAVE *By Richard C. Osborn*

I am a third-generation Seventh-day Adventist. I was raised in what Bill Loveless, my former pastor at Columbia Union College, referred to as an "Adventist ghetto." For me, that meant mission compounds and towns like Loma Linda and Takoma Park. All of my schooling had also taken place in small Adventist schools and at Monterey Bay Academy.

My classes at Columbia Union College reinforced the earlier training I had been given in even greater depth. My teachers were excellent. My college pastor forced me to think about religion for the first time in my life. Our college president, Winton Beaven, challenged us to develop our full potential. Paul Hill, my college choir director, carried us to new heights of excellence.

None of this background prepared me for my first outing into a non-Adventist setting when I started graduate school at the University of Maryland. To get ideas for a thesis topic, I had lunch one day with one of the most respected history professors in the department—a man known not only for his brilliance but for showing concern for his students. When we finished eating, he wanted to know more about me and my religion. I told him about Ellen White, thinking she was one of the most famous individuals in American intellectual history, his specialty. He showed a blank face. I then resurrected from my many years of religion classes the arguments I had been taught about her prophetic gift. In a kind way, he told me of others who had been saying similar things at the same time. My faith began to collapse.

Research tells us that when we develop a congenial relationship with a respected adult, we tend to adopt their ideas. What was I to do? Give up my faith? Blame my Adventist education for not preparing me for this challenge to my belief system?

I had also learned some other important lessons about trusting in the Lord and not just leaning on my own understanding. By acknowledging God's ability to lead me to new understandings, I found a new Ellen White. My new viewpoint was respectful of my heritage but grew into a deeper understanding of God's gift to us. My college experience had helped me weather this potential tidal wave through a trusting relationship with the Lord.

Trust in the Lord with all your heart and lean not on your own understanding. Proverbs 3:5, NIV

Richard C. Osborn is vice president for education of the Columbia Union Conference of Seventh-day Adventists in Columbia, Maryland. He graduated from Columbia Union College in 1969.

THE NAME WE CARRY   *By Sharon Hardwick Leach*

I was a bride of two whole weeks when I arrived at Andrews University to register for my junior year. Getting the classes I needed was easy.

Finding a job proved to be tougher. A job was a necessity. My husband, Benjie, was entering the seminary, and seminary couples are notoriously poor. The only job I could find was as a librarian's secretary, a full-time job that would have precluded going to school. I came home for lunch in tears over my predicament, but my brand-new husband would have none of my dropping out of college. We prayed about it, and Benjie took me by the hand and led me right back to my advisor, Dr. Bill Oliphant, a journalism professor.

"Well . . ." he looked at me, "The PR office is looking for an afternoon typist. Can you type?" (I was grateful that my father had insisted I take high-school typing classes.)

Dr. Oliphant called the PR director, Dr. Horace Shaw, and told him that Sharon Leach was coming about the typing job. I went to his office, introduced myself to Dr. Shaw, and was hired to begin work the next day.

Three months later, the news director—in a deadline panic late one afternoon—asked me to write a short news story. I did; he liked it; they hired a new typist; I wrote news for the next two years; and I found my career in public relations.

At about the same three-month mark, I discovered that college PR offices are extremely responsive to college trustees. It occurred to me that the reason I had been hired initially had little to do with my typing skills and had everything to do with the fact that my father-in-law (albeit of only two weeks at that point) was a trustee of Andrews University.

The blessings we enjoy on this earth and our eternal salvation have nothing to do with our skills or attainments or good deeds. They have everything to do with whose name we carry.

Save me, O God, by thy name, and judge me by thy strength. Psalm 54:1

Sharon Hardwick Leach is vice president for advancement of Southwestern Adventist College in Keene, Texas. She graduated from Andrews University in 1971.

LOVE IN A TEACHER'S CLOTHING   *By Kenneth R. Coonley*

I n 1994, I learned that Elder Robert E. Francis had died. A friend and example I greatly admired was gone.

Twenty-one years before, I had sold my share of a thriving business to enter the gospel ministry. I was thirty-five years old, so when my wife, two children, and I arrived at Southern Missionary College, I was the "old man" in the class of theology students.

I soon heard stories about "REF" and his tough and demanding classroom style. Those stories proved to be true. However, I also soon learned that Elder Francis was a Christian who cared deeply for the students at that college.

Perhaps because of my age, I was asked to monitor the student activities center. Shortly after beginning my work as monitor, I noticed Elder Francis coming in often to play Ping-Pong and table games with the students. I was deeply impressed to see such warm and genuine relationships developing between students and that remarkable man, relationships that would never develop in the same way in the classroom.

On many occasions, late in the evening, his wife, Bea, would call and ask, "Is Bob there at the student center? Please tell him to come home. His supper is cold."

Long after the day's regular schedule of classes was over, and he could have been home, Elder Francis would be with the students, building relationships and having great fun doing it.

No lesson has meant more to me in my ministry than the one Elder Francis taught me: If I really want to influence people and make a difference in their lives, I must be willing to sacrifice, to give of *myself* (even if I miss a meal or two), to be genuine, and to let people know I really enjoy the time I spend with them.

Elder Francis never knew I was watching him, nor did he know how much he influenced my ministry. I wish that I had told him.

My college experience would not have been as fulfilling to me had I not known this totally unselfish Christian teacher and had the privilege of seeing him demonstrate genuine love.

Elder Francis will be missed.

By this all men will know that you are my disciples, if you love one another. John 13:35, NIV

Kenneth R. Coonley is president of the Carolina Conference of Seventh-day Adventists in Charlotte, North Carolina. He graduated from Atlantic Union College (Adult Degree Program) in 1987.

BOMB-SHELTER COMMITMENT *By George W. Timpson*

Twice a day, the enemy rained down deadly destruction upon us during the invasion of Okinawa. Huddled in a bomb shelter, I thought about my status as a dropout from the Seventh-day Adventist academy in Baltimore. I made a covenant with God. If He returned me safely to my home thousands of miles away in Baltimore, I would reenter training in one of our Christian schools. I'd get an education that would benefit humanity and help build His kingdom. I would become an active worker in attempting to turn the hearts of men and women to righteousness.

Safely back in Baltimore, I found that honoring my covenant would be a challenge. My family of thirteen, while surviving the Depression, had moved from the farm to the inner city. I would have absolutely no financial support from them. My military service in the Fighting Seabees provided only limited GI education benefits. How could I honor my bomb-shelter commitment and enter the church's work force?

Abraham's "Jehovah-Jireh" experience, meaning "the Lord will provide" or "the Lord will to *do* it," became a tangible reality for me during this time. I entered the freshman class at Oakwood College in 1947. More than eight hundred students were competing for campus jobs, and was I grateful when I got one on the college farm earning nineteen cents per hour. Before long, I was promoted to supervisor of all the institution's vehicles, considered by some of my envious schoolmates as the top job on campus. I earned maximum pay and had the opportunity to travel to many faraway places.

At graduation, many of my fellow graduates were despondent because they had no job offers. I had *eight*.

Today, many doors of opportunity seem shut toward securing a Christian education or employment. But the God "whom we serve *is able!*" Biblical accounts are very clear: *Our God will make a way!* He will feed His flock. I know there is for each of us a "Jehovah-Jireh" experience. Be prepared to claim it!

Abraham looked up and there in a thicket he saw a ram caught by its horns. He went over and took the ram and sacrificed it as a burnt offering instead of his son. So Abraham called that place The Lord Will Provide. Genesis 22:13, 14, NIV

George W. Timpson is secretary of the Mid-America Union Conference of Seventh-day Adventists in Lincoln, Nebraska. He graduated from Oakwood College in 1952.

DISAPPOINTMENT AND DOGGED FAITH *By Elmer L. Malcolm*

I planned to become a brick mason after graduating from high school. Malcolm Brothers employed college students, so I joined their crew. A year later, a graduate student persuaded me to apply to Columbia Union College.

In the middle of taking the entrance exam, I realized that my high-school preparation was inadequate for college. Overwhelmed, I slipped out of the exam room, unnoticed by the professor. But my student friend persisted. He persuaded the administration to accept me on "condition."

Although I was uncertain about a career, I majored in theology. I took Greek and had a difficult time. But when I finished college, I had taken so much Greek that when I later entered graduate school, the requirement for a second language was waived.

The responsibility for all finances was mine, so bricklaying received most of my energy. Not surprisingly, my grades suffered and I just squeaked by academically.

My senior year kept me very busy planning a wedding, completing a correspondence course, taking regular classes, and working in masonry. I planned to marry on July 22. Then the administration informed me that I had not received proper permission to take the correspondence course and must take summer school with classes beginning one day after the wedding.

The Potomac Conference had already employed me subject to graduation. In shock, I went to see the conference president. He advised me to marry, work to build up a "nest egg," complete the second-semester American history course, and enter the ministry the following summer. So that's what I decided to do.

In a short time, however, that president retired. A new pharaoh was elected, and Joseph was forgotten! My stress level peaked when church policy changed, effectively requiring seminary training before ministerial employment. Now I faced another confrontation with academia. I felt so defeated and small I could have sat on a Kleenex and my feet would still dangle!

Apprehension about seminary soon abated, and I became academically alive. Later, while pastoring full time, I received a Ph.D. from Michigan State University. The struggle with Greek and the seminary detour were unplanned helps to this achievement.

By God's grace, the challenges and disappointments did not diminish my faith in Proverbs 3:5, a text introduced to me by a high-school teacher. I still believe it is an excellent philosophy to live by.

In all thy ways acknowledge him, and he shall direct thy paths. Proverbs 3:6

Elmer L. Malcolm is president of the Northern New England Conference of Seventh-day Adventists in Portland, Maine. He graduated from Columbia Union College in 1957.

CAUGHT IN THE ACT *By Larry W. Boughman*

I had never lived in a dorm before. My roommate and I didn't last long together, which was fine with me. I liked having the room to myself. It was room 104 on the ground floor of Hamilton Hall, near the back entrance. I soon found that I could slip in and out of my room very easily through the window after lights out and visit with my friends.

After one year in college, I went back home to South Carolina to work during the summer. I met a young lady from Tennessee and persuaded her and her parents that Southwestern was the school for her.

Since it was my second year at college, I chose room 104. I liked the room for its location on the ground floor. I tried to decorate the room as best I could. It helped that I still didn't have a roommate.

I wanted to show my girlfriend my room, and I told her it would be very easy to just step through the open window to my room and take a look. We arranged for a time after supper, and she came and stepped through the window and was looking around when someone knocked.

Carol quickly stepped into the closet near the entrance to my room. I opened the door, and there stood the dean. He didn't say a word. He looked around and then opened the closet door, and there stood Carol, eating an apple. I knew we were in trouble, and I was afraid of what was going to happen, especially to Carol.

The dean looked at her and then at me and said, "I don't know what I am going to do, but I will have to do something." Carol and I were waiting each day to be called in for our punishment, but it never came.

I am not sure why the dean never said anything, but Carol and I were married the next summer, and we have never forgotten that experience and the apparent understanding of the dean. Even though we were clearly breaking a rule—a rule that had its own good reasons—he also understood that what we were doing was innocent in itself.

After twenty-eight years of marriage, we still laugh at this experience. But we also realize that special understanding and judgment are necessary when working with young people.

The Lord, the Lord, a God merciful and gracious, slow to anger, and abounding in steadfast love and faithfulness. Exodus 34:6, RSV

Larry W. Boughman is superintendent of schools of the Hawaii Conference of Seventh-day Adventists in Honolulu, Hawaii. He graduated from Southwestern Adventist College in 1972.

PREANSWERED PRAYER *By John Nixon*

Every evening, we claimed the promise of Proverbs 3:5, 6 in prayer before we separated to go to our dorms. I would graduate soon, and my girlfriend and I were sure we were in love.

We had worked hard to build our relationship on a spiritual foundation. We attended chapels and worships together, read the Bible together, and prayed together often. We knew we wanted to marry, but we did not trust our own judgment. So we asked God to direct our path. And we believed He would do it.

Unknown to my girlfriend, however, I had a backup plan.

Secretly in prayer, I regularly asked the Lord to reveal His will in a tangible way. This was a private prayer I told no one about, and I never prayed it aloud. My specific request was that God would show His will regarding our marriage by providing the money we needed to set up a home. I did not request a particular amount of money. I left that to His will. I prayed this each night and waited for Heaven's reply.

One day, I happened to be in the lobby of the dorm when the lobby telephone rang. When I picked up the receiver, I was surprised to hear a familiar voice.

"Johnny, is that you?"

"Mom?! Is everything all right?"

She poured out her news. "Do you remember being hit by a car when you were eleven years old? Well, there was a legal action over that which has been caught up in the system for ten years. It's finally been settled. An attorney called and said you have been awarded five thousand dollars!"

The telephone dropped from my hand, and I almost dropped with it. A flood of emotions overwhelmed me—gratitude, joy, awe, humility, and wonder. God had answered my prayer in a decisive way. He had heard my prayer ten years before I ever prayed it and used the circumstances of an unfortunate accident and a clogged legal system to minister to me in the fullness of time.

That very day, my girlfriend and I became engaged. Four months later, we were married and have been happily so ever since. Our union is built upon the firmest foundation possible. God revealed to us that we belong together. And what God did for us, I know He will do for all who pray in faith.

Trust in the Lord with all thine heart; and lean not unto thine own understanding. In all thy ways acknowledge him, and he shall direct thy paths. Proverbs 3:5, 6

John Nixon is senior pastor of Atlantic Union College Church in South Lancaster, Massachusetts. He graduated from Oakwood College in 1976.

GOOD HABITS THAT PAY DIVIDENDS *By Michael Wixwat*

As an undergraduate, I enjoyed a carefree life. I attended classes and went to work but had no regular schedule for studying. I spent lots of time watching intramurals, and if there was a good basketball game going, I often played until late in the evening. Typically, on my way back to my dorm room, I would drop in to visit my friend Rodney. We'd get absorbed in a long conversation about some of the scenery around campus. Finally, about the time my roommate wanted to go to bed, I would begin to study or work on whatever assignments were due the next day. Not surprisingly, my grades were very average.

Then I graduated and worked for a year. When I went back to Andrews to get my master's degree, I was engaged to Melanie. She had much more structure to her life. Because I wanted to be around her as much as possible, I began to adjust to her disciplined life. Whenever I had a spare period, I could usually find her studying in a library cubicle. Soon I formed the habit of studying in the library in the evenings just to be with her. During that year of graduate school, I discovered that I never had to study after nine o'clock in the evening, and I got much better grades.

Good habits do pay off. Of course, I hadn't intentionally worked to develop good study habits. I just wanted to be near Melanie. But my motivation didn't really matter. The end result was scholastic success.

The same is true in my spiritual life. Every day, I must set aside a time to study God's Word. This time must be a good time in my day when my energy levels are high. For me, that means the morning. I have found that my spiritual life suffers if I miss my morning time with God. He is not concerned with what my initial motives are for spending time with Him. He will be happy to commune with me, and I will find that the end result is spiritual success.

In the morning, O Lord, you hear my voice; in the morning I lay my requests before you and wait in expectation. Psalm 5:3, NIV

Michael Wixwat is secretary-treasurer of the Minnesota Conference of Seventh-day Adventists in Maple Grove, Minnesota. He graduated from Andrews University in 1983.

SAVOR THE MOMENT By David Merling

During college, I was invited by W.C. Neff and the Stitzer, Wisconsin, SDA Church to conduct my first evangelistic campaign. Elder Neff treated me like a son. He was the epitome of a Christian gentleman and my association with him has only made me a better minister.

The church members were enthusiastic. They handed out invitations, actively helped during the meetings, and faithfully attended. Elder Neff and I visited those who were interested. Each night I preached the best that my inexperience allowed.

In the end, two elderly women were baptized. Although outwardly I expressed pleasure in their decision for Jesus, I was disappointed that so much effort had produced so few baptisms.

After the meetings I returned to school for the fall quarter with two resolutions: 1) to do well in my studies; and 2) to never conduct another evangelistic meeting.

About two months after school started I received a letter from one of the women who had been baptized. She thanked me for coming to Stitzer and told me how pleased she was to meet my family. The real purpose of her letter, however, was to tell me that she had just learned she had cancer and had only a short time to live. She wrote that she was so happy that she had learned the wonderful truth of Jesus before she died.

Her letter changed my opinion of the effort that had gone into those evangelistic meetings. Somehow it did not seem too much for so little anymore.

From this experience I have tried to learn not to allow unrealistic expectations or anticipated difficulties ruin an otherwise pleasant experience. I could, and should, have enjoyed the event of that woman's baptism as much when it occurred as I did later, when confronted with her death. It was a matter of savoring the moment.

When God finished the creation of the world, He could have begun fretting over the problems to come, but He paused to savor the moment and pronounced that what He had made was good (Genesis 1:31). In college we endure rules that impose on our freedoms. We can focus on our expectations and allow them to rule our attitude or we can savor the moment. It is surprising how often even the worst events of the present are blessings of the future.

And God saw all that He had made, and behold, it was very good. Genesis 1:31

David Merling is assistant professor of archaeology and history of antiquity at the Seventh-day Adventist Theological Seminary at Andrews University in Berrien Springs, Michigan. He graduated from Southern College in 1974.

WHERE THE PROBLEM ISN'T *By R. Ernest Castillo*

Very well do I remember when my parents helped me become the proud owner of a 1959 Chevy. It was an old car, and I was not at all mechanically inclined. At least I did know how to start it, where the gas and brake pedals were, and how to shift the gears. But that was about all.

I felt so proud. Now I could pick up my girlfriend, who lived with a family off campus. No longer would I have to ask others for a ride, for myself or for her. *I had a car!*

One day, while I was driving back to campus after dropping my fiancée at the home where she was staying, the car began to sputter. I quickly pulled off the road and parked. The engine quit. I tried different things to start it again, but to no avail. It was apparent to me that my old car had given up the ghost. With great discouragement, I made the long walk back to my dorm on campus!

The following day, my mechanically minded roommate drove me back to my car. He took his out his toolbox and worked under the hood for a while. Finally, he looked at me, and with a big grin on his face, he asked,

"Does this car have any gas in it?"

Sure enough, we had been trying to solve a problem where the problem really was not.

Many times in our Christian experience, even as college students, we try to serve God while relying on our own efforts. We think that struggling to obey His law and perform the duties of the Christian life will earn us our salvation. Ellen White says of this, "Such religion is worth nothing" (*Steps to Christ*, 44). When we think that securing our salvation is dependant on doing these things, we are fighting where the battle isn't. Jesus is our salvation, and because of who He is, we will work to live up to His standard. But it is His fulfillment of that standard, not ours, that brings us our salvation.

Submit yourselves, then, to God. Resist the devil, and he will flee from you. James 4:7, NIV

R. Ernest Castillo is secretary of the Pacific Union Conference of Seventh-day Adventists in Westlake Village, California. He graduated from Pacific Union College in 1970.

A VICTIM BUT NOT A CASUALTY By *Jim Epperson*

His name was Kenny. He stood five feet tall and weighed about ninety-five pounds. If he could have straightened up his crippled, twisted body, he probably would have stretched to six feet. His shriveled legs dipped together at the knees to form an inverted "V." His feet shuffled and flopped as he maneuvered down the halls, making an eerie sound that suggested a desperate struggle for survival. When Kenny spoke, his voice came out in a slurred whining sound, barely audible at times and difficult to understand most of the time.

Kenny was a victim of multiple sclerosis—a victim, but not a casualty. In spite of the monumental physical problems he faced each day, Kenny had risen above them all. He had learned not to dwell on his differences. He ignored the embarrassed gazes and the nervous acknowledgments of those he met. More significantly, he didn't blame anyone for his plight. Nor did he view his handicap as an obstacle to his goals and aspirations of life.

Kenny was never late for class because he began shuffling across campus fifteen or twenty minutes ahead of everyone else. The lights in his room were the last to go out at night and the first to come on in the morning, because it took him three times as long to complete a written assignment. Yet his work was always done on time.

One of Kenny's goals was to get a date for the senior honors banquet.

After a great amount of self-persuasion, he asked the desired girl to accompany him to the banquet. She was devastated, embarrassed, and exasperated. Should she accept or turn him down? Unwilling to do either, she faked being sick to avoid the decision.

Why didn't Kenny get despondent after this embarrassing putdown? How did he keep from cursing God for his plight? Kenny would respond: "If God could make man from the dust of the ground, He can make me anything He pleases. And if I give Him all that I have, He can transform me into a miracle."

Kenny found another date for the banquet. And he graduated from college Magna Cum Laude. He was a miracle.

The Lord God formed man of the dust of the ground, and breathed into his nostrils the breath of life. Genesis 2:7

Jim Epperson is director of education of the Southern Union Conference of Seventh-day Adventists in Decatur, Georgia. He graduated from Walla Walla College in 1965.

GOOD PUBLIC RELATIONS *By Lori Tripp Peckham*

When I returned to the dorm one afternoon, I found a message on the board: "Call Dr. Chase."

I dialed his number, wondering what the chair of the communication department wanted.

"Hello," he greeted me. "St. Helena Hospital has requested a public relations intern this quarter. I think you would be perfect." He explained that I would get practicum credit and asked, "Can you report to the director of public relations tomorrow?"

I agreed and the next afternoon found myself walking into Mr. Barnett's office in the basement of the hospital. He motioned for me to have a seat and told me all about public relations and what he would like me to do during my time there.

He ended by saying, "I'm sorry we don't have an office for you. We'll set up a desk in the office of our director of publications, Kim Peckham."

Before I left, Mr. Barnett took me on a tour of the department. When he led me into Kim's office, I was surprised to see a handsome, friendly young man.

Hmmm, I thought. *This is going to be fun.*

As I spent time with Kim, a recent graduate of Union College, I grew to respect and like him more and more. Not only did I learn about public relations that quarter but I learned how easy it was to talk to him about good books and God's leading in people's lives.

When my internship ended, we exchanged addresses, and I headed to La Sierra for graduate study. The next two Christmases we exchanged cards, and then two years later Kim looked me up on a visit to southern California.

Over brunch at Lake Arrowhead, we found ourselves remembering our conversations in the basement of St. Helena Hospital and sharing how God had led us since. And this time we didn't say goodbye for long—we found God leading us to employment at the same place, and over the next few years we dated and married.

When I chose to attend an Adventist college, I hoped that along with finding a career and close friendships I would meet my future husband. And it happened—the very last quarter of my senior year and not in the way I expected. But when God does things, they always turn out right.

Delight yourself in the Lord and he will give you the desires of your heart. Psalm 37:4, NIV

Lori Tripp Peckham is editor of Insight *at the Review and Herald Publishing Association in Hagerstown, Maryland. She graduated from Pacific Union College in 1984.*

TRACTOR LESSON *By Dan Matthews*

To help pay my way through college, the Lord blessed me with a variety of jobs that all turned out to be valuable learning experiences in themselves. I worked at carpentry, masonry, logging, shoveling coal, mining, and farming, besides some attempts at sales.

One vital life lesson came on the driver's seat of a farm tractor. Driving a tractor itself was not complicated. And plowing a field sounded easy enough. The main point was to plow a straight furrow. I was told this would happen if I selected a point at the other end of the field and drove straight toward it by aligning it with the radiator cap on the front of the tractor.

It all seemed easy enough until I became more eager to see how straight the furrow was than to keep my eye fastened on the goal point at the other end of the field. After only a brief backward glance, I had to correct the steering wheel to get back on course.

At the far end of the field, I turned to prepare to plow another furrow from which the soil would be laid against the upturned soil from the first furrow. Looking along that first furrow, I could see exactly where I had looked back and had to correct my direction.

Anyone who has ever plowed a field and carelessly looked back as I did knows how difficult it is to "cover your mistake" and try to get things lined up again in a proper way.

This simple life lesson took on special meaning when I studied how to preach with practical application and appeal. My Homiletics teacher at Walla Walla College was Elder Gordon Balharrie. He was a master teacher and preacher. He knew how to inspire us to mine Scripture for a revelation of God's understanding of our human inclinations and actions.

During one of Elder Balharrie's classes, our study passage focused on Luke 9:62. "No one, after putting his hand to the plow and looking back, is fit for the kingdom" (NASB). Elder Balharrie coupled Hebrews 12:2 with Luke 9:62.

He encouraged us to look to Jesus in all of life's experiences. "Never look back, and the kingdom is yours."

Fixing our eyes on Jesus, the author and perfecter of faith. Hebrews 12:2, NASB

Dan Matthews is speaker/director of the Faith For Today *television broadcast in Simi Valley, California. He graduated from Walla Walla College in 1957.*

INTELLECTUAL INTEGRITY *By Richard Fredericks*

During my first two years of college, I did the "fresh-out-of-academy-restrictions, immature, selfish-pig, party-animal" gig.

Like many in that mode, I justified all my actions by loud railing against the hypocrisy of religion. But by my junior year, the railing about the irrelevancy of God was wearing thin. Shallow relationships weren't much fun anymore. The pressures of adulthood were making their first inroads. A good friend had been killed in a drinking accident and another crippled for life. My family was in trauma, and my own shouting about the self-sufficient life was ringing hollow in my soul.

Another thing was happening. Friends were becoming Christians—not just Adventists, as in members of a denomination—but Christians, as in disciples of the risen Christ. I ridiculed them, but they courageously held to their convictions.

One day, I said something sarcastic about the Bible. A new believer popped his cork and said to me, "If you really had any intellectual integrity, you wouldn't open your mouth until you'd read it for yourself." "OK," I said, "I will." And I did. I read the New Testament through in a couple of weeks.

There were no fireworks or epiphanies. Nothing specific clicked. But I sensed my need to dig deeper. I started through again. Then it happened. On the lawn in front of Weiss Library. I was alone on a sunny day, plowing through Romans. I came to the verse below—and it clicked.

God suffered for me, to forgive and give me identity. God broke into history and died the death I deserve, for my sins, to take my guilt away and to give me the reality of a meaningful, high-impact life with Him. Life meant more than maximizing pleasure and minimizing pain. At the center of the universe, there isn't cold chaos, but a Heart that beats warm with sacrificial love for us.

The real adventure began that day. I accepted the Gift and found joy in the journey. If this hasn't happened for you, and religion is still just about paying dues and keeping rules, then I encourage you to encounter the Christ of the cross. He still waits for honest seekers.

God demonstrates His own love for us in this: While we were still sinners, Christ died for us. Romans 5:8, NIV

Richard Fredericks is pastor of Damascus Seventh-day Adventist Church in Damascus, Maryland. He graduated from Columbia Union College in 1975.

THE MIND SET FREE By Walter Scragg

I was writing, furiously writing. If I could play back his words in a few weeks' time, college would be a breeze. Then my thoughts stumbled, and my pen faltered, skidded, and stopped.

Lionel Turner, Avondale College's most popular teacher, wasn't pouring out facts for me to record and replay. This was New Testament Synthetics, and *he was asking questions*. Questions about why Paul said this and not that. About what "oneness" meant in Ephesians. What it meant to be "one in Christ."

My mind struggled. It craved the comfort of answers, not the uncertainty of questions. If college would push me into this kind of intellectual world, I didn't want it.

My close friends, Bob Wilson and Graham Miller, their eyes glazed over, stared in undisguised bewilderment as the flow of questions went on and on. Across the aisle, George Laxton, another buddy, was doodling his way to the end-of-class bell.

How could Dr. Turner do this to me? Didn't he know the answers? And what if I answered his questions the wrong way? Did his questions mean that he didn't believe? Shouldn't he affirm rather than query? Hadn't I come to college to learn facts? What good did it serve to buzz with questions?

Escape from Turner's relentlessly questioning mind wasn't possible. I looked ahead to three more years, and he taught at least one required subject each year.

That first week at college, I opened my Bible with different eyes. This was not the Bible of church and Sabbath School, with lists of texts to prove this and that. Ephesians was a whole, not a gathering of proof texts. Paul had purpose and direction as he wrote.

I read and reread what my father wrote in the Bible he gave me that day I left for college. "Study to shew thyself approved unto God, a workman that needeth not to be ashamed, rightly dividing the word of truth" (2 Timothy 3:15). This was what Dr. Turner wanted of me!

Would my faith survive? Would I ride out the winds of new ideas to a safe haven? Thoughts tumbled this way and that.

And then, my racing mind screeched to a halt. If my teacher had asked himself these questions and still loved God's Word and its Lord, as he clearly did, then I, too, might safely search and expect faith and not doubt.

Study to shew thyself approved unto God, a workman that needeth not to be ashamed, rightly dividing the word of truth. 2 Timothy 2:15.

Walter Scragg retired in 1995 as president of Adventist World Radio at the General Conference of Seventh-day Adventists in Silver Spring, Maryland. He graduated from Avondale College in 1945.

GRAD-SCHOOL MISSIONARY By *Russell Staples*

When I enrolled as a graduate student in anthropology at Princeton University, I learned what it was like to be regarded as an absolute curiosity because of my religious profession.

My time at Helderberg College in South Africa had confirmed my discipleship, and I had become a missionary in Central Africa. At Princeton, I was studying systematic theology, but because of my missionary career, I persuaded my advisors to allow me to do some work in anthropology. And so there I was ("a real, live missionary" was the word that went around) among the anthropology students. I was nicknamed "The Missionary."

And even professors who were, of course, too formally correct to address me that way could hardly suppress a discreet smile at the reference.

At times when critical issues regarding religion arose, somebody was bound to say, "Ask the missionary; he ought to know."

Topics were assigned for student papers in a seminar on social theory soon after I joined the program. During this process, a group of students rather forcefully requested that I be assigned a certain topic. Moltmann's book *Theology of Hope* had burst upon the American academic community like a flaming meteor. The case he made for the function of religion in society ran directly counter to contemporary sociological assumptions, and the clamor was for me to analyze his thesis. Was his vision of the church really a possibility? I protested that this belonged to the realm of sociology of religion and not anthropology, but my protests went unheeded. The topic was deemed relevant and assigned to me.

In due course, I presented the paper, expecting vigorous and even harsh criticism. Discussion was lively, but as we proceeded, I sensed a softening. Some even allowed that social life would, in fact, be beautiful if it reflected the values of the gospel. In the end, much to my surprise, I was criticized for failing to make the case boldly enough.

As time went on, I found that I was expected to defend the Christian enterprise when it came under attack and that my classmates felt let down if I did not. This reminded me of the response of the Athenians to Paul on Mars Hill. Some scoffed, but others said, "We will hear you again about this" (Acts 17:32. RSV). Some of my classmates scoffed, but most were of the latter class. In spite of themselves, they wanted to hear again and again. Deep down in the human heart is a hunger that responds to the message you and I can share if we can get over our reticence.

You are the light of the world. A city on a hill cannot be hidden. . . . Let your light shine before men, that they may see your good deeds and praise your Father in heaven. Matthew 5:14-16, NIV

Russell Staples is professor emeritus of world mission at the Seventh-day Adventist Theological Seminary at Andrews University in Berrien Springs, Michigan. He graduated from Helderberg College in 1945.

GIVE ME TEN MINUTES MORE
By Robert G. Peck

Freshman Composition was my most difficult class. And one-third of my grade for the semester was riding on the final two-hour exam.

The first hour was to be objective, and the final hour required an in-class theme. Writing a five-hundred-word theme was extremely difficult for me and always took *hours* to complete. I knew it would be impossible for me to write a rough draft first, as the professor required, and then write the final draft in ink and hand it in by the time the bell rang.

But that was the assignment. The teacher made it clear that when the bell rang, we were to put down our pens and immediately hand in the ink draft.

How well I remember that day. I finished the objective part of the test within the allotted time. Then I faced the theme. The professor assigned the topic, and my mind went blank. For twenty minutes, I sat immobilized, unable to write a word. Perspiration broke out on my forehead as I began to panic.

I put my head down on the desk and prayed. I reminded God that He had called me to the ministry and I would have to prepare sermons. If I couldn't even write a five-hundred-word theme, perhaps I should accept the scholarship I had been offered to a state university for a business administration degree.

At that very moment, my mind flooded with thoughts and ideas for my theme. I couldn't write fast enough to keep up. By the time I finished my rough draft, only a few minutes remained to write the final ink draft, not nearly enough time to complete it. What could I do? I did the only thing possible. I prayed that the bell wouldn't ring until I finished writing the final draft. I needed about ten more minutes beyond the end of the period.

As I wrote, I heard the clock on the tower at the administration building strike the hour that normally ended that test period. But in the building where I was taking the test, the class bell didn't ring. *The bell simply didn't ring that hour!* The professor, apparently waiting for the bell, didn't call for the papers. I wrote for ten more minutes, finished the final draft, handed in my paper, and got a "B" for the course.

In a way highly impressionable to my young mind, God heard my prayer. His action increased my faith in Him, in my calling to the ministry, and in His ability to provide for my future. I still praise Him today for the bell that never rang.

Trust in the Lord with all thine heart; and lean not unto thine own understanding. In all thy ways acknowledge him, and he shall direct thy paths. Proverbs 3:5, 6

Robert G. Peck is president of the Dakota Conference of Seventh-day Adventists in Pierre, South Dakota. He graduated from Union College in 1971.

WILL THE REAL GOD PLEASE STAND UP? *By Penny Shell*

Perhaps I just was born feeling guilty. At least by the time I reached college, I was pretty good at it. God was more often the avenging judge than the prodigal parent. So that's where Miss Shull comes in.

As a college freshman, I was quite proud of getting into Miss Shull's two-hour English class instead of the more elementary three-hour class. I was, that is, until I realized how much harder it was, how much more writing was involved, and how much discipline was necessary to crank out the assignments. One week when affairs of the heart had kept me consulting with dorm mates late into the night instead of studying and sleeping, I had to face my own inadequacy. It was the day writing assignments were due; it was the hour for class. In a panic, I tried to beat out a paper on my old portable Olivetti. Nothing worked. I finally dashed to class paperless and late—about as bad as it could get by my view of Miss Shull's standards. Others handed in papers. Not I.

With her usual no-nonsense face, she said to me, "I'd like to see you in my office after class." College students who have perpetrated worse offenses can't conceive the terror I felt during that agonizing class period.

Miss Shull gave us an assignment to work on in class and then consulted with students individually. I couldn't concentrate. I thought of running out the door. I thought of the shame to my family, the shock of my classmates if my guilty secret became known. How would I face my judge at the end of class?

With a martyr's resolve, I approached her office when the bell rang.

"Miss Shell," she began, "I made some cookies today, and I thought you might like to share them with your friends." I couldn't speak. My relief was as warm and sweet as those fresh-baked chocolate-chip cookies. The zapping God began to crumble, and the real God reached out to me in that moment. Perhaps few understandings bestowed in college are more important than that. Perhaps few pictures of God are as powerful as the teacher who cares because—just because that's who she is.

Do not fear, for I am with you, do not be afraid, for I am your God; I will strengthen you, I will help you, I will uphold you with my victorious right hand. Isaiah 41:10, NRSV

Penny Shell is chaplain and manager of pastoral care services for Shady Grove Adventist Hospital in Rockville, Maryland. She graduated from Union College in 1962.

A CALL, A CATTLE FARM, AND COLLEGE By Stephen Orian

Midway through my junior year at Thunderbird Academy in Arizona, I deeply sensed that God was calling me into pastoral ministry. So when I graduated in 1968, there was no question in my mind that I would enroll at La Sierra College in the fall to begin my ministerial course.

Two weeks after graduation, my family moved to Arkansas and invested all the family savings in a chicken and cattle farm. La Sierra College suddenly was 1,200 miles farther away. Worse, it now was financially out of reach.

A few weeks into the summer, I learned about another Adventist college about 375 miles from my new home on the farm. It was called Southwestern Union College (now Southwestern Adventist College). I was not impressed. Even if I had been, and even though it was closer to home and a little lower in tuition than La Sierra, there was still no money for tuition. My summer work on the family farm, earned me no paycheck. Dad had already borrowed heavily to get the farm going.

Soon fall came. It was time to begin college and my preparation for the ministry. Yet it seemed to me the door had slammed in my face.

The University of Arkansas in Fayetteville was only twenty miles away, but of course, it didn't offer a theology degree. I reluctantly enrolled, trying to get a start on some college work. "Lord," I prayed, "why is this happening to me? I sensed Your call. I still sense Your calling. So why am I enrolled in this state university?"

All during that freshman year, I dreamed of attending La Sierra College. "Maybe next year," I told myself. Yet by the time my sophomore year began, I knew that dream would never be a reality. I continued at Fayetteville. The summer before my junior year, I prayed, "Lord, I've already taken virtually all my prerequisites at this state university. I must begin taking the religion classes necessary for the ministry—even Greek! And besides Greek is a two-year course! If I don't start it this year, it will take an extra year for me to finish college and begin my ministry."

That very summer, I saw the Lord open door after door for me to attend an Adventist college. Interestingly, He also opened the door of my mind to consider Southwestern Union College. Somehow I had been prejudiced against the school, feeling my preparation there would be very inadequate. When I finally enrolled, reality proved to be just the opposite!

The Lord had His plan for my life. That became very evident as I saw His leading, in spite of the obstacles that seemed to make His call of no avail.

O Lord, thou art my God; I will exalt thee, I will praise thy name; for thou hast done wonderful things; thy counsels of old are faithfulness and truth. Isaiah 25:1

Stephen Orian is secretary of the Arkansas-Louisiana Conference of Seventh-day Adventists in Shreveport, Louisiana. He graduated from Southwestern Adventist College in 1972.

OUT OF CONTROL By *Joel O. Tompkins*

"Girls' dorm! Girls' dorm! Girls' dorm!" came the raucous chant as I cautiously walked through the front door of the men's dormitory. Suddenly with the noise came hordes of young men bursting out of the hallways, down the stairs, and past me out the door. The mob spirit was in full form as the men vocalized their intentions.

It was my freshman year at Southern Missionary College, and this type of activity was new to me. I followed along, asking, "Why are we going to the girls' dorm?"

"We're gonna have some fun tonight!"

The large crowd sprinted across the campus to the other dormitory. The women eagerly awaited us, streaming out onto the second-floor porch as the frenzied dean quickly locked all entrances to the building. Someone started the singing with a tune that was popular on the hit parade of the time: "Come On a My House."

There we were—two crowds of human beings yearning to get to each other. Several faculty members, hearing the commotion, slowly drove by, observing the action. A few of the young men hurried over to the street and lifted the rear end of one of the cars. I will never forget the look of fear on that teacher's face. We were nearly out of control.

After a short time, the men's dean, Mr. Everett Watrous, in his usual kind and wise way, spoke to all of us. "Fellows, you have had a good time tonight. Now let's sing 'Good Night, Ladies' and go on back to the dorm." Our adrenaline spent, we sang the song, and like innocent little puppies followed him meekly back to the dorm.

That experience made a profound impression upon me! A while later, I discussed our actions with others who had taken part, and we admitted to each other that we had been *controlled by the wrong spirit. We would have done anything that night!*

I have thought of that experience many times since, shuddering to think how unsafe it is to be void of the Holy Spirit for even a moment. What a privilege Christians enjoy!

"The soul that is yielded to Christ becomes His own fortress, which He holds in a revolted world. . . . A soul thus kept in possession by the heavenly agencies *is impregnable* to the assaults of Satan. But unless we do yield ourselves to the control of Christ, we shall be dominated by the wicked one" (*The Desire of Ages*, 324).

I will pray the Father, and He will give you another helper, that He may abide with you forever, even the Spirit of Truth . . . , for He dwells with you and will be in you. John 14:16, 17, NKJV

Joel O. Tompkins retired in 1995 as president of the Mid-America Union Conference of Seventh-day Adventists in Lincoln, Nebraska, and chairman of the board of Union College. He graduated from Southern College in 1955.

A GRAB FOR GLORY By *Charles C. Case, Sr.*

While showering after a vigorous flagball game at La Sierra College, I noticed a tiny bulge on my lower abdomen. I worried it might be a hernia. Two weeks later, the doctor confirmed my suspicion.

The injury continued to enlarge, and during Christmas vacation I had surgery. Because I was in such good physical shape, I went home from the hospital in two days, but in great pain when I walked.

Three weeks passed, and I went back to school, still recovering from the surgery. Academy Seniors Day came, when more than four hundred high-school seniors came to the college for special recruiting programs. I was a member of the college's performing gymnastic troupe and decided to perform my special trampoline routine. I knew it would please the crowd—and it did. I performed flawlessly. The visitors really liked my high, full-layout back flips.

After the gymnastic show was over, I went back to Calkins Hall, my dormitory, and called my parents about the day. They scolded me for my poor judgment in performing before I was fully recovered from my injury. As I accepted the scolding, I realized that my parents were right. They had spent a lot of money for the surgery, and I could easily have blown it. The surgeon later told me that if I had torn the internal repairs, they would have been very difficult to fix. My trampoline performance, a self-centered grab for glory, had really been an exercise in foolishness.

I took my parents' counsel and stayed off the trampoline for several weeks before resuming my routine. Over the years, I realized what a "dumb" decision I had made, just because I wanted to make a great public impression.

God has to deal with us spiritually, even in our "dumb" decision making. Often, our poor decisions are motivated by self-glorification. He doesn't want one of us to perish, so He patiently waits and works for us, helping us to grow out of our spiritual immaturity and foolishness.

I am thankful that I did grow up spiritually and that God waited and worked for me. Although I still may make some unwise decisions, I understand what to do and where to go.

The way of a fool is right in his own eyes, but a wise man listens to advice. Proverbs 12:15, RSV

Charles C. Case, Sr., is president of the Southern New England Conference of Seventh-day Adventists in South Lancaster, Massachusetts. He graduated from La Sierra University in 1954.

ASSURANCE FOR A COUNTRY BOY *By Lester Carney*

During my first year of college, an incident occurred that I have shared with very few others in the intervening decades. Yet the memory of it has been a source of comfort and an anchor to my faith.

Like many others entering college in the early 1950s, I had to work very long hours to earn my tuition and stay in school. Early in my freshman year, I worked so much that I did not have adequate time for study, and my course load was heavy: Bible Doctrines, Freshman Composition, American History, and Greek. Within a few weeks, I realized that I was failing all of my courses except American History.

One morning, I knelt for my usual prayer in my dorm—room 222 in old North Hall at what was then Washington Missionary College (now Columbia Union College). I was deeply concerned about the unfortunate state of my academic life. As I prayed for God's help and guidance, something unusual happened. It is difficult to explain, because it almost seemed like a dream; as if I had fallen asleep.

I saw a figure, encircled with light, suspended between the floor and the ceiling in the window area of that old dormitory room. My attention was first drawn to the feet. Then slowly I raised my view up the robed figure. The image faded away before my gaze reached the face.

I do not try to make many explanations of this experience. I only know that from that day on, everything turned around in my life. My mind seemed able to comprehend things more easily, and my grades improved dramatically. Never again did I find myself failing any college or university class. To me, that experience seemed that God was giving assurance to this young country boy of His presence and care. It has been a precious source of strength to me over the many years and different phases of my ministry.

Lo, I am with you alway. Matthew 28:20

Lester Carney is president of the Manitoba-Saskatchewan Conference of Seventh-day Adventists in Saskatoon, Saskatchewan. He graduated from Columbia Union College in 1955.

PUSHING THE FRONTIERS *By Ray Dabrowski*

My college days taught me that true religion does not lie in organized and solemn demonstrations of piety and that Adventism has a meaning only if it instills hope into the commonplace.

A personal reflection, if you please.

The Sabbath service was over. A long line of worshipers filed out of the sanctuary. As the preacher of the morning, I greeted the saints on the way out. Handshakes. Smiles. I accepted the simple "thank-you" and the profound "I was challenged."

Then he and she appeared. Said she: "Do you remember us? We went to college together." They left me no choice but to admit that I remembered going to college but that I didn't remember being there with them. An apology is always a virtue.

Some fifty handshakes later, she spoke again: "I will never forget those days in college. You were always on the move and constantly challenging the status quo. Who would've imagined seeing you preach on Sabbath morning."

Impressions. I didn't mind her reminding me of those challenging days when our Adventist academic milieu was uncomfortable with tough questions of the day—the war in Vietnam, academic freedom, cultural diversity. I didn't mind her being surprised that I was holding an open Bible in my hands.

Memories. Though baptized a number of years earlier, it was during college when my faith was tested and reestablished. Though recollections are dim, yet I remember what went on at our basement apartment at 122 Hillcrest Drive. The music we listened to was alternative. Decent folks wouldn't have approved of the late hour of the night, either. They wouldn't have approved of the culturally challenging debates. We all knew then that life was about pushing frontiers. And this is what we did at Andrews.

Everyone loved Gottfried Oosterwal.

Why? Well . . . he had something to say to us. And he listened. And didn't mind sitting on the floor and listening to Robert Johnson's blues tapes. Or, as the rumor had it, he would disappear for a few days to experience life in a hippie commune. The *mystique* was there—an ingredient of acceptance and affirmation.

It was the *listening* versus *hearing* that made a difference in my life then. A teacher, who cared to listen and hear what was a part of my soul. A philosopher, whose book on the Sabbath gave a meaning to my own Sabbath keeping. They gave a caring reason why one was richer by being a believer and why believing is to go beyond the tried and true—to establish in the world a need for justice, for peace, for love, for dignity, for hope.

They were all bigger than the "Don't do that!" of the establishment.

So, what was my college-faith road like? It was a journey to discover the principles and virtues that make life meaningful. My college days gave me an affirmation of the need to reflect that the *here* and *now* has a meaning only if it immersed in the hope for a future with Christ.

He has showed you, O man, what is good. And what does the Lord require of you? To act justly and to love mercy and to walk humbly with your God. Micah 6:8, NIV

Ray Dabrowski is communication director of the General Conference of Seventh-day Adventists in Silver Spring, Maryland. He graduated from Andrews University in 1975.

THE LORD WILL MAKE
A WAY SOMEHOW!
By J. Alfred Johnson II

The approach of registration for spring quarter of my junior year at Oakwood College filled me with dread. I was out of money. Student loans, which had carried me this far, were gone, and the campus work-study program would not provide enough.

Knowing that all my resources were gone, it was particularly painful when excited classmates asked what courses I was going to take spring quarter. With no rich relatives to call on, my only resort was to prayerfully, though reluctantly, consider doing college by correspondence.

I dutifully went to my job in the development/alumni office and told a co-worker of my plan to leave Oakwood. I noticed, while I was talking, that Mrs. Angela Wilson, the president of Oakwood's alumni association, was in deep concentration at her desk. A few minutes later, she called me to her desk, handed me a folded note, and instructed me to take it over to the Financial Aid Office.

The reader may guess what happened during my walk to that other office. Curiosity got the best of me. The note read "The National Alumni Association will pay all expenses for J. Alfred Johnson II for the Spring Quarter of 1972."

I jumped for joy and shouted all I wanted to! The Lord had come through for me in a big way! Through His continued blessing, I graduated on schedule with the class of 1973—with a credit in the business office!

The God we serve is "an equal-opportunity Blesser!" I guarantee that what He did for me, He can do for you. Hold on! The Lord will make a way, somehow!

My God shall supply all your need according to his riches in glory by Christ Jesus. Philippians 4:19

J. Alfred Johnson II is president of the Central States Conference of Seventh-day Adventist in Kansas City, Kansas. He graduated from Oakwood College in 1973.

COVERED BY HIS WINGS
By Ciro Sepulveda

We woke up that Thanksgiving morning in 1969 attempting to put on a happy face, but without much success.

We could hear and see our neighbors going about their affairs, full of laughter and smiles. The Thanksgiving spirit at Andrews University seemed to permeate the air outside. But it couldn't penetrate the walls of our efficiency apartment.

Gloria and I, newlyweds, had finished school at La Sierra College in the winter of 1968. We had stuffed our little Fiat with all our belongings, till there wasn't an inch of space left. With the savings of a lifetime, $800, we drove from Riverside, California, to Berrien Springs, Michigan.

At Andrews, our plans quickly ran into roadblocks and dead ends. After hearing our case, the business manager devastated our idealism by suggesting we climb back into our Fiat and return to California. He said that in the wintertime at Andrews, jobs were hard to find and apartments scarce. When we mentioned our $800, he discovered an empty efficiency apartment. That afternoon, both of us found jobs in the furniture factory.

Within a year, the $800 had vanished. We were loaded down with loans, enough to last us a lifetime, it seemed. When the second Thanksgiving at Andrews arrived, our refrigerator sat empty. The thirty-six cents in the house could not begin to buy a Thanksgiving dinner.

I began to question whether this was the will of God. Maybe we should have listened to the business manager a year and a half earlier? Maybe the ministry was not what God wanted for me? Maybe I committed a grave error by taking those loans? Maybe the fact that all my classmates at La Sierra got sponsorships to Andrews and I did not had been a signal from God that I had blindly ignored?

In the middle of that Thanksgiving afternoon, the smell of fresh bread, mashed potatoes, gravy, and cranberry sauce crept through our door from the other apartments. Someone knocked at the door. I opened it and stared into an empty hall; no one in sight. About to close the door, I glanced down and saw two shopping bags full of groceries.

Our dinner that day was wonderful. But the feeling that we were not alone; that God had not forgotten us; that we were still covered by His wings, made that Thanksgiving our best.

He will cover you with his with his feathers, and under his wings you will find refuge. Psalm 91:4, NIV

Ciro Sepulveda is vice president for student services of Atlantic Union College in South Lancaster, Massachusetts. He graduated from La Sierra University in 1968.

GOD'S CALL AND APTITUDE TESTS   *By Ted Wick*

As an academy junior, I committed my life to Christ. I thought that meant committing my life to Him as a minister.

So when I arrived at Union College, I was clear about my life's work. But that was before I took Freshmen Orientation, a two-hour class in which we endured every aptitude test then available. After the tests, I met with the professor to discuss my results. Basing his opinion on those results, he made it clear that I should plan on another line of work. It was devastating news, but I believed him. Who was I to challenge those tests made by professionals?

I dropped all my preministerial classes for second semester and enrolled only in what might be useful for pre-medicine or pre-architecture.

Lowell Welch, the dean of students, called me in for a visit during this confused period of my life. "I am disappointed in you," he said. "I thought you were going to become a minister!" I explained what had happened on my aptitude tests. I expected a pat on the head for being a good boy and listening to my elders. Instead, he pressed on: "Most ministers I know had to overcome some challenge in order to answer the Lord's call. In fact, how could a minister effectively help struggling people if he hadn't had any difficult experiences himself?"

Now I was more confused than ever. How had I gotten derailed? Why had I doubted my earlier sense of God's call?

I made a deal with the Lord. I had two big problems: money for the following year's tuition and confusion about my professional goals. If God would help me sell enough Christian books during the summer to earn a full colporteur scholarship, I would take that as His confirmation of my call to ministry.

I spent many days that summer leaning heavily on the promise of Isaiah 41:10. And by summer's end, I had my confirmation. With a full scholarship in hand, I returned to college, enrolled in beginning Greek, and never looked back.

Do not fear, for I am with you; do not be dismayed, for I am your God. I will strengthen you and help you; I will uphold you with my righteous right hand. Isaiah 41:10, NIV

Ted Wick is director of the Office of Volunteers for ADRA International, at the General Conference of Seventh-day Adventists in Silver Spring, Maryland. He graduated from Union College in 1959.

A PRICELESS
TWENTY-FIVE-CENT LESSON *By Jay Gallimore*

Paying for Christian education surely wasn't easy for the Gallimores. Mother insisted on staying at home when her boys were young, so she didn't take an outside job until we were in academy. My father got a late start in life because of his four years of service in World War II.

My parents became Adventists when I was six and my brother was three. As a result of their determination and dedication, we never spent a day in public school. My parents weren't always sure where all the extra tuition money would come from, but their faith in God and their diligence were rewarded by seeing both their sons through graduate school.

While I attended Southern College, my mother would send me two dollars a week for personal items. I spent it carefully. One day, some friends asked me to contribute twenty-five cents for a friend's birthday surprise. I readily agreed and then discovered, to my embarrassment, that I had only thirteen cents.

Now this was a *very* small problem. Should I bother the Creator of the universe with such a thing? As I walked around the Collegedale shopping center, I sent up a prayer asking God to help me with my problem. On my way back to the dorm, I realized that I needed to do my part. So—I began watching the ground.

It was a long walk across the open lawn to Jones Hall. I saw nothing. I started up the stairs to the third floor. I saw nothing. At the top of the stairs, it hit me like "a bolt from the blue." I must go to the prayer room directly across from the stairs and look under the cushion of the chair. I did.

There, to my amazement, was a quarter. I knelt there and thanked the Lord for His answer to my very small need. And I never found another dime under the cushion of that well-used chair!

That seemingly insignificant experience is really quite significant in my life. At a formative time in my development, I viewed it as an obvious, direct answer to a simple, honest need. It helped prepare me to meet far greater challenges and see God answer other, bigger prayers in some awesome ways.

Three lessons from that small experience have stood me well over the years. First, God cares about the little things. Second, I must ask. Third, I must exercise faith, by acting on my request.

Do not be anxious then, saying, "What shall we eat? or What shall we drink?" . . . for your heavenly Father knows that you need all these things. Matthew 6:31, 32, NASB

Jay Gallimore is president of the Michigan Conference of Seventh-day Adventists in Lansing, Michigan. He graduated from Southern College in 1970.

THE GOLDEN RULE REVISITED *By Lolethia Kibble*

"Roommate, you missed it! Church was great, and lunch was too," Janice chirped as she bounced into the room.

"Leave me alone," I snapped at my unsuspecting roommate. Without explanation, I abruptly turned to face the wall and continued nursing the headache that had kept me in bed all morning.

As I turned, I caught the pain in her eyes. Immediately, I knew I was wrong. My natural impulse was to apologize, but pride would not permit it. *I was the one in pain*, I rationalized. Would I ask her to pretend she was well if she was not? NO! "Do unto others as you would have them do unto you." Thus I justified my rudeness. For years, I remained troubled by the incident.

One way the golden rule can be interpreted is: meet the needs of others as you would have them meet your needs. People are different and have different needs. There are four temperament types: the confident choleric, the calm phlegmatic, the warm sanguine, and the reflective melancholy. The calm phlegmatic, who is often indifferent, can easily hurt the reflective melancholy with a careless remark. I must not only recognize tempera-ments, but fulfill the needs mandated by those temperaments.

Twenty years later, God placed Janice and me together again. I was happy for the opportunity to apologize. With some trepidation, I recapped that Sabbath afternoon. Graciously, she said, "I don't really remember." Did she "really" forget, or was she meeting *my* need?

Whatsoever ye would that men should do to you, do ye even so to them. Matthew 7:12.

Lolethia Kibble is superintendent of schools of the Allegheny East Conference of Seventh-day Adventists in Pine Forge, Pennsylvania. She graduated from Oakwood College in 1964.

BURNED OUT *Benjamin D. Schoun*

The pattern developed in college. Out of bed for that 7:30 class. Oops, skip class to study for that quiz at 8:30. Then rush to the library to get those books for my term paper. Then chapel, another class, lunch, SA com-mittee, work. I became so busy that I began to postpone the important things in order to do the urgent ones.

I understood that the important things related to values, and for me they included my spiritual life, my family life, friends, and my health, among others. But I said to myself, "I can lose some sleep and overwork for a short period of time. I've got to get these urgent things done! But when I gradu-ate, things will be different!"

When I graduated, I found myself very busy. But I said to myself, "I'm just getting started in my career. I have to work hard and get organized. After I get started, it will be different." And my important priorities were slighted.

My work had a way of growing. New tasks and responsibilities were added. I kept finding reasons for postponing my priorities. I finally began to real-ize that I was in a trap. It *wasn't* going to be different. I became disillu-sioned, wondering if the struggle was worth it. I finally burned out and quit my job as a pastor. I considered changing my career.

Only when I firmly reordered my priorities under the guidance of God did I begin to be renewed. Things began to *be* different. I went back to pastoring with a new pattern. I learned that a priority is only good for the present. It loses its essence when it is put off.

Start living now, even in college! Balance your life with your important priorities. One of the beautiful promises of Scripture is that God is eager to help us with our priorities by giving us "singleness of heart and action."

They will be my people, and I will be their God. I will give them singleness of heart and action, so that they will always fear me for their own good and the good of their children after them. Jeremiah 32:38, 39, NIV

Benjamin D. Schoun is associate dean of the Seventh-day Adventist Theological Seminary at Andrews University in Berrien Springs, Michigan. He graduated from Andrews University in 1970.

SLEEPWALKERS, AWAKE! *By Jerry N. Page*

During my academy and college years, reality to me meant struggling to be free from the rules, traditions, and confines of the Adventist Church and educational system. I wanted out!

I had spent eighteen years living in the home of an Adventist preacher and teacher and attending Adventist churches and schools. None of that had led me to a real understanding of a living relationship with Jesus or the assurance of salvation we can have in His family. After being kicked out of three academies and entering the sixties drug culture in full force, I wanted to attend a state college and be free.

My parents loved me and used the "financial incentive" to get me to attend one year at Union College. After that freshman year, I enrolled in a pre-law business major at a state college in Denver. During the next year and a half, as I roared full speed into many new experiences, my parents intensified their efforts too. I think they must have called everyone they knew across North America, asking them to intercede for their boy, Jerry, to have his eyes opened. But I was like a sleepwalker, thinking I was aware, but oblivious to a better, brighter reality.

The Lord allowed me to become continually more miserable as my relationships deteriorated from selfishness. It was a dark period. I was earning good grades but feeling sick when faced with future self-centered careers; I was getting high but ending up emotionally low.

I praise God that on a Saturday night in 1971, after a bad drug experience, my girlfriend and I talked of hating people. We ended up deciding to commit our lives to the Lord, whose unconditional love we had experienced from Christians around us.

After that initial awakening, I felt the call to pastoral ministry and enrolled at Andrews University. There, the Lord awakened me to the power of small-group ministry, outreach activity, claiming Bible promises, and the true assurance of salvation. More than twenty years later, I'm realizing Jesus will give us daily spiritual awakenings if we will let Him!

I am sending you to them to open their eyes and turn them from darkness to light, and from the power of Satan to God. Acts 26:17, 18, NIV

Jerry N. Page is president of the Central California Conference of Seventh-day Adventists in Clovis, California. He graduated from Andrews University in 1973.

HEAVENLY PLACES *By Kenneth A. Strand*

Some fifty years ago, a newly converted Seventh-day Adventist youth turned down a scholarship at a secular university and trekked off to Walla Walla College. This school soon seemed to him to be a bit of heaven on earth. Why?

This experience is mine, and several things quickly contributed to my feeling of being in a heavenly place: my first Bible class, Life and Teachings of Jesus; the evening worships in West Hall (long since demolished) with dean of men Leon Losey commenting on passages from *Steps to Christ*; and last, but not least, fellowship with teachers, students, and work supervisors who reflected the image of Jesus.

In the Bible course, we were required for every class session to memorize a Bible text and a passage from *The Desire of Ages*, *Christ's Object Lessons*, or *Thoughts From the Mount of Blessing*. Not only did this sharpen my memorization skills (a blessing in its own right), but also—and more significantly—it fortified my mind with a broad spectrum of Bible texts and Ellen White statements that have been helpful ever since. One example is from *Desire of Ages*, page 429: "Cast yourself at His [Christ's] feet with the cry, 'Lord, I believe; help *Thou* mine unbelief.' You can never perish while you do this—never."

My delightful months at Walla Walla College were interrupted by my father's suffering a heart attack and my own need for more money to continue college. I moved to the Midwest, where I worked several years and then resumed my studies at Emmanuel Missionary College (Andrews University) in Berrien Springs, Michigan. There, I again felt that I was living in a bit of heaven on earth. Among the flood of happy memories from my student years at EMC, my association with Dr. Edwin R. Thiele, my major professor, especially stands out. Dr. Thiele's research achievements, including his solution to the chronology of the books of Kings and Chronicles—a problem that had baffled great scholars for more than two millennia—and his consistently strong faith inspired in me a confidence in God's Word that no doubtings of critics could ever efface.

"Heavenly places in Christ Jesus" is, of course, the daily experience of all true followers of Christ. But to me in my earliest years as a Seventh-day Adventist, the heavenly atmosphere of two college campuses gave special meaning and encouragement.

God, who is rich in mercy, . . . [has] made us sit together in heavenly places in Christ Jesus. Ephesians 2:4-6

Kenneth A. Strand is professor emeritus of church history at the Seventh-day Adventist Theological Seminary at Andrews University in Berrien Springs, Michigan. He graduated from Andrews University in 1952.

ONE LESS QUESTION *By G. Edward Reid*

The summer after my college sophomore year, I sold Adventist books in eastern Kentucky. On the very last day of my summer's work, I was in an automobile accident that probably changed the course of my life.

My car was a beautiful 1956 Chevy convertible with a new metallic blue paint job and a new white top. And now it was totaled. I wasn't hurt badly, but as I stood by the side of the road waiting for the tow truck, I couldn't help asking God why this happened to me.

I had given an entire summer to God's work. It was my last day of deliveries, and I was excited about going back to college and seeing my friends. Now I was standing beside my wrecked dream car with a deep cut over my left eye and blood running down my face and onto my tie and white shirt.

Some problems in life we can understand now. Other mysteries will only be solved in heaven when we can ask God for an explanation. I couldn't understand this problem.

A friend from school took me back to Collegedale, and instead of arriving back on campus in my special car, I was on foot. I had been dating a nice girl who was not a student at the college, and I had planned to continue the relationship by going to see her as often as I could in my convertible. Not surprisingly, that relationship languished without that car.

Later during that year, I bought an older, 1951 four-door sedan called by my friends "the bean brown Chevy." I also began praying that God would lead me to the "right person" for my life companion. The following summer, I joined one of my teachers and several classmates in a field school of evangelism. During that training program, I decided to sell the "bean brown Chevy" and buy a more representative car for my senior year and my entrance into the ministry.

At the dealership, I found a new 1966 Chevy Chevelle and decided to buy it. While completing the paperwork for financing and insuring the car, I was assisted by an Adventist girl whom I had admired at college but had never dated or even met. Now she had a summer job in this car dealership. Because I had no prior credit history, the financing process took a rather long time. While waiting for the approval, I got up the courage to ask the young lady for a date, adding that she would get to ride in the new car.

That was twenty cars ago, and she has ridden in every one of my new cars since.

So now I have one less question I will have to ask God when we get to heaven. Instead of a question then, I only have praise now.

The secret things belong to the Lord our God, but those things which are revealed belong to us and to our children forever. Deuteronomy 29:29, NKJV

G. Edward Reid is stewardship director of the North American Division of Seventh-day Adventists in Silver Spring, Maryland. He graduated from Southern College in 1967.

A MAN WITHOUT A DIME *By Billy E. Wright*

My parents would have helped pay for my college education, but I decided to do it on my own. So it was no surprise that I arrived at Southwestern Union College in 1967 *without a dime in my pocket.*

I had no idea what the quarterly tuition would be. I simply showed up intent on fulfilling a commission from God to become a minister. He had called me from Prairie View A & M College, where I had been majoring in electrical engineering. I felt strongly that since God obviously wanted me at Southwestern, it was up to Him to provide a job and the money I needed to receive the necessary training.

Immediately upon my arrival, the Lord found me a job at Brandom Kitchens. The pay was great but not enough to cover my total school bill. Even a loan from the state of Texas didn't meet the need. But I didn't worry. I had learned to trust God.

Sometimes the old enemy of the soul—Satan—tried to sow the seed of doubt in my mind about God's power to meet my needs. I rebuked him in the name of Jesus. I said, "Get behind me! God will provide as long as I trust in Him!"

I claimed many Bible passages during this time. One of my favorites was James 1:5, 6, where we are instructed to ask for wisdom with complete faith and trust. I lived by the code "Trust God, no matter how dark the night!"

Many times I saw students sent home from college for lack of money to pay their school bills. I, too, was behind on my bill, but I didn't worry. I reminded God that He had called me to Southwestern and that I was depending totally upon Him to provide the means to keep me there.

Without fail, God always provided what I needed. One time I was called to the business office. I dreaded going, because I had exhausted all possible sources of tuition money. Bracing myself for the inevitable bad news, I prepared a good speech about why I couldn't be sent home—I was on a mission for God.

I never got a chance to make my speech. The financial advisor told me that someone had deposited money on my account. I left that office praising the Lord! I served a God who did hear and answer prayer.

Another time, when I thought I'd have to give my speech, the financial advisor told me that I had pay left over from a job the year before. I told him there must be some mistake, because I had received all my pay. Despite my arguments, he insisted that the credit be applied toward my bill. Of course, I left the office praising the Lord and thanking Him for yet again increasing my faith and trust in Him.

Ye have not chosen me, but I have chosen you, and ordained you, that ye should go and bring forth fruit, and that your fruit should remain: that whatsoever ye shall ask of the Father in my name, he may give it you. John 15:16

Billy E. Wright is secretary of the Southwest Region Conference of Seventh-day Adventists in Dallas, Texas. He graduated from Southwestern Adventist College in 1970.

SABBATH EXAMS By Ray Mitchell

S abbath exams. Nasty thought! For Seventh-day Adventists it's practically an oxymoron. *Sabbath* brings to mind such happy memories of rest, worship, refreshment, and fun with family and friends. *Exam* evokes tension, stress, and judgment.

I studied science at a public university in Sydney, Australia. The University of New South Wales found that the easiest day to set an exam that wouldn't clash with other classes was Saturday. Because regular classes were never scheduled on that day, many of my exams were.

I needed Sabbath exams like a submarine needs a screen door. My Sabbaths were precious. They kept me sane. Since then, I've really learned to love to worship and focus on God and the things that matter to Him. Back then, I simply appreciated the break. I was so glad He had asked us not to work on Sabbath. And by any definition, taking an exam on Sabbath was work to me.

I decided the university authorities had to hear about this injustice. "Protest!" was my plan. "Religious discrimination!" would be my war cry.

Their response? "We have lots of students who won't write exams on Saturday. You may take the tests with them after sundown for $50." So I spent many Sabbaths under the supervision of a university staff member from the beginning of the regular exam time until after dark, when I took an exam.

I never regretted it. My friends could not understand what I was doing. "If I had to wait twenty-four hours after studying to take a test, I would fail," said one. But I never failed one Sabbath exam. To be honest, there were times I thought I would. But I always felt a special blessing was upon me for obeying God.

As a zoology major, it was my way of saying, "I honor God as the creator of all things. I rest today because He asked me to remember that I am made in His image." He was always faithful to His promise, "Those who honor me I will honor" (1 Samuel 2:30).

If you call the Sabbath a delight and the Lord's holy day honorable, and if you honor it by not going your own way and not doing as you please . . . then you will find your joy in the Lord, and I will cause you to ride on the heights of the land. Isaiah 58:13, 14, NIV

Ray Mitchell is senior pastor of Pacific Union College Church in Angwin, California. He graduated from the University of New South Wales in 1970.

ELEPHANT STAKES By Larry Evans

College was a crossroads experience for me. I was forced to come to grips with the question, "Who am I—really?"

I'll never forget the day during my senior year in high school when a visiting school counselor told me I would not make it in college. He had looked at my grades and concluded that the past was a forecast of the future. I almost believed him.

What he did not know, however, was that I had just experienced a spiritual conversion that changed my whole outlook on life. That experience changed not only my attitude but also my aptitude for learning.

Many of us have struggled with our identity. Without a scriptural reference point, we will be limited by what our culture, parents and friends have told us. Someone once asked a circus trainer how a ten-ton elephant could be staked down with the same-size stake as a young three hundred-pound elephant.

"It's easy," he answered, "if you know two things. Elephants really do have great memories, but they aren't very smart. When they are babies, we stake them down. They try to tug away from the stake perhaps ten thousand times before they realize they can't possibly get away. At that point, their 'elephant memory' takes over—and they remember for the rest of their lives that they can't get away from the stake."

The Bible proclaims that in Christ we have a "fresh start"! Translated, that means my personal "elephant stakes" don't have to be permanent. That's one of the reasons the gospel is such good news!

Our firm decision is to work from this focused center: One man died for everyone. That puts everyone in the same boat. . . . Because of this decision we don't evaluate people by what they have or how they look. We looked at the Messiah that way once and got it all wrong, as you know. We certainly don't look at him that way anymore. Now we look inside, and what we see is that anyone united with the Messiah gets a fresh start, is created new. 2 Corinthians 5:15-17, The Message

Larry Evans is president of the New Jersey Conference of Seventh-day Adventists in Trenton, New Jersey. He graduated from Walla Walla College in 1970.

PIZZA, SPINOZA, AND EPIPHANY   *By Clifford Goldstein*

In the late 1970s, I was a student at the University of Florida in Gainesville. At that time, the only Adventist I knew was a guy I smoked pot with at the local gas station where I worked to support my sky-diving habit.

One evening, in an Italian grease pit across from the school, I sat eating a pizza, drinking a beer, and reading Stuart Hampshire's classic work on Spinoza. My eyes latched onto a sentence that in one brief, epiphanic moment changed my life forever.

Though I was raised in a Jewish home, my folks rejected religion long before my birth. My father's belief in God ended when he was among the first troops who liberated Dachau at the end of World War II. So I was reared on post-modernist relativism, which meant, essentially, that no absolutes—whether ontological or ethical—existed. Reality was a subjective experience, and morality—all in your head.

But what I read that evening claimed something to the effect that in order to live the most perfect life, one needed to find out the reason why he was here and then live accordingly. Those words sliced into me like a prefrontal lobotomy. They instantly wiped out the relativism that I had been nurtured on. Suddenly, it struck me: "Hey, I exist, this pizza exists, and so somewhere out there, an objective truth had to correspond to and explain the objective reality that I am a part of!"

Just as the pizza and the pepperoni on it had to come from somewhere, so did I. This meant that there had to be an explanation for existence both transcending and independent of my own subjective comprehension of reality. And that explanation, whatever it was, was truth.

Now this all might seem Mickey Mouse for a guy in his early twenties, but it contradicted the whole worldview on which I had been raised. Because reality existed, truth must too! How could I have missed it?

That evening, I left the restaurant and walked through the quiet, dark streets of Gainesville, back to the library. As never before, my heart burned with a desire to know truth, if it were humanly possible to *know truth*. For though I now realized that truth had to exist, the limitations of human knowledge might keep me from it. But I wanted to know it, no matter the cost.

Little did I know what that cost would be. But a few years later, I found it, in Jesus Christ.

Ye shall seek me, and find me, when ye shall search for me with all your heart. Jeremiah 29:13

Clifford Goldstein is editor of Liberty *at the General Conference of Seventh-day Adventists in Silver Spring, Maryland. He graduated from the University of Florida in Gainesville in 1978.*

GRACE ENCOUNTER *By W. G. Nelson*

During my sophomore year at Atlantic Union College, I was, at best, an erratic scholar. As a history major who intended to pursue a career as a teacher, I nonetheless suffered from sporadic lapses of academic focus. Sometimes I skipped class to engage in "important" alternative activities. And of course, on those days I was careful to avoid the teachers of those skipped classes. I didn't want to face their well-intentioned inquiries about my most recent absence.

One morning, after skipping my U.S History class, I had an errand in the administration building. I rounded a corner, and there, walking briskly toward me, was my history professor, Dr. John Christian. I had no chance for a graceful detour. "Hello, W. G.," he greeted me. "I have been looking for you." My worst fears realized, I braced myself for the inevitable. "I am going to have an opening for a reader next year," he continued. "You have done well on my essay tests, and I wondered if you would consider working for me?" Dumbfounded, I could only mumble an inarticulate thanks and make an appointment to discuss the offer in more detail later.

The spiritual ramifications of this encounter were not lost on me. I have pondered them often since. My behavior justified a reprimand. I expected disapproval or even condemnation. Instead, I was invited to experience a deeper fellowship. My teacher had chosen to affirm my potential rather than dwell on my shortcomings. I had been the benefi- ciary of grace, unmerited favor. I had caught a glimpse of the gospel in action.

Since we have been justified through faith, we have peace with God through our Lord Jesus Christ, through whom we have gained access by faith into this grace in which we now stand. Romans 5:1, 2, NIV

W. G. Nelson is president of Walla Walla College in College Place, Washington. He graduated from Atlantic Union College in 1972.

HE GUARDS THE WAY *By Don J. Coles*

After academy, I really intended to go to college. But good work was so plentiful that I postponed college for a while.

Twelve years later, and thirty years old, I finally went to college. It wasn't easy. I had a family now, and I was leaving the vice-presidency of a plywood plant. Sitting in a classroom taking assignments required all the discipline I had.

My freshman Bible class, called Biblical Philosophy, required that I learn key texts and Spirit of Prophecy quotes. I had to read the Bible through, and then, on the basis of the content of each book, answer the question "What kind of person is God?"

Anybody could do this, but it required a lot of thought. Was God portrayed as stern and demanding, or was He a loving Father wanting the best for each of us?

Some passages were for Israel of long ago, but I found many promises that apply to life today. I saw one such promise fulfilled in a dramatic way during the summer between my freshman and sophomore years.

I still had ties to the lumber industry, so I took a summer job in the rugged mountains of northern California helping to build logging roads into the timber. The work site was 325 miles from my home and family at Pacific Union College, so I was on the job during the week and made the long drive home and back on the weekends.

The road into the remote work area was narrow, crooked, even dangerous, with no shoulders or guard rails in many places. I knew the road well and drove my VW Bug at maximum possible speed.

One Sunday, while roaring up that winding road to the work site, I heard a voice say, "Don, slow down." It wasn't an audible voice as such, but it might as well have been. The demand on my conscience was so strong that I braked hard, slowing to 20 miles per hour.

Puttering, now, around the next corner, I suddenly faced two huge logging trucks bearing down on me. One truck was passing the other and had not quite accomplished this when I rounded the corner. There was no place to go to avoid a head-on collision. We skidded to a stop just inches apart. With the extra speed I had been traveling at before I heard the voice, my little car, with me in it, would certainly have been smashed against that big truck.

That experience showed me that God is indeed a loving Father meeting our needs. He had truly sent His angel ahead of me to guard the way. The principles I learned in that freshman Bible class are still meaningful today.

I am sending an angel ahead of you to guard you along the way. Exodus 23:20, NIV

Don J. Coles is a trustee of Pacific Union College in Angwin, California. He graduated from the same institution in 1963.

THE 150-POUND WEAKLING *By Dick Duerksen*

The telephone voice was insistent. "Hurry, Chaplain. We need you in the emergency room. Now!" I grabbed my Spanish Bible, gasped a quick prayer, and dashed down two flights of stairs to meet the day's next challenge.

Being a student missionary was like being hit with surprise midterms several times a day. The screams met me before I touched basement. Male and female voices locked in shrill condemnation and terror. He stood on the left, barely restrained by two emergency-room technicians. She screamed unendingly from the right. Between them lay the broken and lifeless body of their only child, eight-year-old Jose.

"This never would have happened if you had obeyed me! He wasn't to ride his bike on the street!"

She cringed at her husband's anger and then screamed all the louder. "I didn't know he was outside! I was only away for a minute!"

Pablo's voice shouted above the din, "Dick, help me!" Pablo Garcia was a burly E.R. technician, a wrestler who was losing his grip on the angry husband. I was a 150-pound weakling. A scared weakling, clutching a Bible and wishing I were home in Greek class.

All my theology training flashed through my head, followed by quick bursts of General Psychology, American History, and Homiletics. No answers jumped from the video. And the screaming continued.

"Psalm 23. Read Psalm 23." The voice in my head seemed strangely calm in the chaos. "Now! Read the shepherd's psalm."

I obediently fumbled open my Bible and began to read.

"Jehová es mi pastor." Pablo's face was incredulous. He had ordered another wrestler and got a psalm instead.

"Nada me faltará." The struggling stopped.

"Aun cuando ande por el valle de la sombra de muerte." The screaming turned to sobs.

"Y en la casa de Jehova moraré para siempre." They were in each other's arms, repeating the words with me.

The third time through, there were four voices softly speaking the words of hope. Four hearts at peace, ready to dwell in His house, today and forever.

The Lord is my shepherd . . . and I will dwell in the house of the Lord forever. Psalm 23

Dick Duerksen is vice president for creative ministries of Columbia Union Conference of Seventh-day Adventists in Columbia, Maryland. He graduated from La Sierra University in 1969.

ZEAL MEETS CALCULUS By Larry Ray

"How did you do on your GREs?"

That was the most agonizing question any classmate ever asked me. A bottom-quartile score in your major field is not something you want to broadcast—particularly when friends are excitedly talking about scores above nintieth percentile. What could I say?

Since my junior year in high school, my dream was to be a math teacher. Helping teenagers learn math was the career I wanted. Certainly, I was destined for it. I had graduated at the top of my high-school class and had four years of college-preparatory math. Understandably, my confidence was high.

So high, in fact, that I bypassed the freshman math course at Pacific Union College. My advisor gave special permission to start immediately in calculus and computer programming. What an ecstatic feeling to be a freshman among sophomores and juniors.

And what a mistake! Without that fundamental freshman math course, I simply wasn't ready for calculus and the other advanced courses. My understanding always lagged one course behind. Advanced calculus during my junior year was pure agony. Without the professor's special mercy, a final passing grade would have been impossible. A later course in algebraic field theory brought me to my knees and almost convinced me to change majors.

Now, after four hard years as a math major, I was faced with a GRE score that would not recommend me for master's work. Had I gotten ahead of God by rushing into calculus as a freshman? In my zeal, had I failed to listen to His voice? Or was math teaching the wrong career for me, and all this trouble was simply God's way of showing me?

I prayed for direction. Teachers and family suggested going ahead with my career plans while starting an in-depth review of college math. I did get a job as a high-school math teacher, and during that first year, I reviewed persistently in preparation for retaking the GRE. Teaching during the day was stimulating; nightly review was painful. But God blessed my efforts. My GRE results the second time showed a remarkable turnaround.

My math major led to a career in education, where I have experienced the exhilaration of helping students plan their programs and master their subjects. When they are down, I remember the agony of my first GRE score. Do I recommend a math major? Yes. Do I recommend skipping a basic course? Usually not.

It is not good to have zeal without knowledge, nor to be hasty and miss the way. Proverbs 19:2, NIV

Larry Ray is vice president for academic administration of Union College in Lincoln, Nebraska. He graduated from Pacific Union College in 1964.

THOSE BEAUTIFUL MORNINGS *By Leo S. Ranzolin*

Nineteen fifty-two was a trying year in my life. After the Lord had reassured me of a career in the ministry, the bottom fell out of everything. My colporteur ministry was a failure. I broke up with my girlfriend. I had no money to continue my education. As I looked at the beautiful rolling hills of our college in Brazil, I was crying inside. The treasurer had just told me that I should go home and work with my father as a truck driver. Perhaps I could come back the following year.

But I wanted to *stay*. Sensing my inadequacy and my fragility, I turned to the Lord. There was, in those days, a beautiful wooded area at the college where the young people would go and pray every Sabbath morning. I joined what was called the *Culto da Mata* (the Worship of the Woods), not realizing at the time that it would have tremendous influence on my Christian life.

Of course, there were other spiritual activities on campus. We had dorm worships and the requisite chapels. There were Friday-night sermons and the Sabbath activities. But the *Culto da Mata* was something very special for my personal spiritual development. Early Sabbath morning, before breakfast, we would meet in the woods. We would sing, and then one of us would speak. It was there that I learned to preach. We would separate in different trails for meditation, come back to the circle, and march toward the cafeteria singing and praising God.

I will never forget those beautiful mornings, going down into the dim woods with our flashlights and then returning up the hill in the sunlight for breakfast. It seemed to me as though I was marching to heaven.

It was during this time that the Lord, through one of my teachers, opened up the door for me to stay at Brazil College and start my degree in theology.

From this experience, I learned, as a young adult, how much I need the Lord every day in my life. It prompted me to memorize verses of the Bible and get involved in the youth programs of the college. As a result, my passion became knowing more about the Lord and His Word. This led, eventually, to a career in youth ministry in the Adventist Church.

I can understand today why the disciples came to Jesus and asked, "Lord teach us how to pray." It is the sine qua non of the Christian life, without which we cannot fellowship with God.

Do not be anxious about anything, but in everything, by prayer and petition, with thanksgiving, present your requests to God. Philippians 4:6, NIV

Leo S. Ranzolin is general vice president of the General Conference of Seventh-day Adventists in Silver Spring, Maryland. He graduated from La Sierra University in 1958.

TRUTH IN THE NIGHT *By Peter van Bemmelen*

In high school in the Netherlands, I had to study the usual subjects—mathematics, biology, history, physics, ancient and modern languages. But I learned little about the meaning of life. Reared in a secular home, I knew practically nothing about Christianity, the Bible, or faith in God. My father, a university professor, called himself an agnostic; my mother was somewhat religious but never went to church. Prayer was unknown in our home.

At age nineteen I entered the University of Groningen to study law. I found it disappointing. It certainly did not provide answers to the questions uppermost in my mind: Why did I exist? What was the purpose of life? Where did we come from? Why was there war, sickness, suffering, and death? I had been taught to believe that life had evolved over millions of years to ever higher stages. Each individual existence, however, had only relative significance, and at the end, death was inescapable. It all seemed rather senseless to me. Yet somehow I came to believe that there had to be purpose to life, but I did not know what it was. I was searching for meaning but could not find it.

The answer to my search came suddenly and unexpectedly. One night early in 1955, I could not sleep and started to read a book entitled *The Truth Shall Make You Free*. For the first time in my life, I was consciously confronted with basic biblical truths: the world and human beings were created by God, and they had not evolved over millions of years; suffering, sickness, and death had resulted from the disobedience of our first parents and were not random byproducts of an evolutionary process; best of all, God would restore humanity and the world to their original condition through His Son, Jesus Christ. I did not lay the book down until I had finished reading it. I believed what I read. Suddenly, life began to make sense. I started to study the Bible and accepted Christ as my Saviour. Two months later, I was baptized.

That special night is now more than forty years ago. God has guided me to become a minister, a missionary, and a teacher. He gave me a wife, children, and grandchildren. I still thank Him for that night when He revealed to me the true meaning of life.

The truth will set you free. John 8:32, NIV

Peter van Bemmelen is professor of theology at the Seventh-day Adventist Theological Seminary at Andrews University in Berrien Springs, Michigan. He graduated from Newbold College in 1959.

OBSTINATE FAITH *By Rodney Applegate*

I stared in shock at the transcript the registrar slid across the counter. Mrs. Pauline Koorenny stated the obvious as kindly as possible. "You have five Withdrawal 'Fs' from the college you previously attended. We have no choice but to place you on scholastic probation."

"It can't be . . . I didn't fail those courses," I stammered. "I was in the hospital from a car accident . . . the school told me everything was taken care of . . . then I got drafted . . ."

Mrs. Koorenny sympathetically helped me face my dilemma and suggested some solutions. But it was clear. My classes had not been properly dropped during those tough times. Now here I was, eager to pursue a theology degree at La Sierra College and finding myself on the edge without failing a test or even being given a chance!

I stumbled through the thicket of students and out of the office, sure that neon arrows were blaring: "loser, Loser, LOSER!"

What should I do now? "Give up," the devil taunted as I beat a retreat to the parking lot and climbed into my old '55 Volvo. Doubts and fears swirled around me like dead, crunchy leaves. "Get a job. Earn some money. At least it will save you the embarrassment of failing."

It would be so much easier, I brooded, *if a quick solution would appear out there in the sky*. But no plane roared by dragging a message from God. All I got was just a quiet and unmistakable impression that fall afternoon: La Sierra College was where God wanted me to be. Scholastic probation didn't have to be forever. Deficits could be erased by excellence. I would hand my faith and my life to Him and focus on putting "As" in the place of "WFs."

God honors faith. Obstinate faith, which looks to Him when we are pressed. College isn't always clear sailing. When the devil tempts you to give up your faith, be obstinate. Tell him, "I'm letting Christ take over!"

Now I take limitations in stride, and with good cheer, these limitations that cut me down to size—abuse, accidents, opposition, bad breaks. I just let Christ take over! 2 Corinthians 12:10, The Message

Rodney Applegate is president of Walla Walla General Hospital in Walla Walla, Washington. He graduated from La Sierra University in 1963.

HOUSE HUNTING By Gil Plubell

Finally, I had landed a job to teach after graduation. My wife and I made a quick trip to settle on housing just before I was to report for duty in August. In our youthful innocence, we had allowed only two days for this important task.

We examined house after house without any success. During the second day, the record of our futile search and the August heat of more than one hundred degrees began taking a toll. Our spirits wilted as disappointment mounted.

But we had to find a place to live—today!

In the middle of the afternoon, we stopped for a lemonade to cool off and assess our options. And we prayed earnestly for help. Back in the car, we wondered what we should do next. Suddenly, the same thought came to both of us, *Go back to the new housing development we visited yesterday.* But why should we do that? We already knew we couldn't buy one of those houses. We had no down payment, and the monthly payments were more than we could afford on my teacher's salary. We needed to rent, not buy.

When we drove on to the construction site, we found the place deserted. All the workers had left for the day. We parked in front of a house that was nearing completion and walked in through the doorless entry, just to look around.

In a flash, a red Buick convertible pulled up in front of the house. A man jumped out of the car, breezed into the house, and immediately asked if we were interested in buying a home.

"Where did you come from?" I asked. "I didn't see any cars around."

"I was just driving down Main Street when I saw you pull in here and stop. I thought you might be interested in buying."

We explained that we had no down payment and were really looking for a place to rent.

"Hey, maybe I can help you. I had a couple in here this afternoon who would really like to buy a house. But they just put down deposit money and signed a rental agreement for a house in town. You could probably take over their rental agreement, and they could buy a house."

Immediately, we contacted the other couple. They readily agreed to the idea, and we had our rental home.

I pondered the goodness of our God and why He would work out such a miracle of timing on our behalf. We were fresh out of college and at the beginning of our teaching ministry. I believe God wanted to tell us something important at that critical time. He wanted us to learn, in a most remarkable way, that He would be there to guide and direct in all our ways, if we would put our trust in Him.

Commit thy way unto the Lord; trust also in him; and he shall bring it to pass. Psalm 37:5

Gil Plubell is director of the office of education, K-12, of the North American Division of Seventh-day Adventists in Silver Spring, Maryland. He graduated from Pacific Union College in 1954.

A DOCTOR IN THE HOUSE *By J. Mailen Kootsey*

Dr. Jim Woody and his family entered our life when we were in graduate school. He came to our university campus to do a residency in pediatrics. Our families shared many meals and social occasions together.

Then they moved on to another city when his program was completed.

Months later, we had a telephone call from Dr. Jim. He was planning to attend a professional meeting on our campus. He asked if he could stay at our home one night. Of course!

On the day of Dr. Jim's visit, our three-year-old son, Brenden, attended a birthday party for one of his friends. Usually cheerful, Brenden came home in a fussy mood, so we put him to bed early, hoping that extra rest would restore his good disposition.

In the middle of the night, my wife and I were awakened by loud crying from Brenden's bedroom. Checking on him, we recognized no warning signs except an apparently stiff neck, but Brenden continued to cry. We decided to try to make him comfortable and take him to see his doctor in the morning.

Then we remembered Dr. Jim. In our sleepy haze, we had forgotten our guest, but he was a doctor and a pediatrician too. Dr. Jim came quickly and placed skillful hands on Brenden. In a calm voice, he said, "Get Brenden to the emergency room as fast as you can go!" We obeyed without question. As we left the house, he phoned ahead to let them know we were coming.

We had been at the emergency room with Brenden before, and a lengthy wait was usual, but not this time. Within thirty minutes, he had an X-ray and a spinal tap and was receiving a massive dose of antibiotics. The diagnosis: bacterial meningitis, frequently fatal.

After a two-week stay in the hospital, Brenden made a full recovery. The doctors said a delay of a couple of hours would have cost him his life or his intelligence. His prompt arrival at the hospital gave the antibiotics a chance to get ahead of the lethal bacteria. Although we didn't know it at the time, the Master Physician had made plans in advance to return a university friend to our home on one specific evening to save our son's life.

Your Father knows what you need before you ask him. Matthew 6:8, NIV

J. Mailen Kootsey is vice president for academic administration of Andrews University in Berrien Springs, Michigan. He graduated from Pacific Union College in 1960.

GREEN GIANT
AND THE SABBATH *By Don F. Gilbert*

For several years, my wife and I had earned our college tuition by renting a farm and growing cash crops. One of our crops was sweet corn for the Green Giant Canning Company. The company provided the seed and set the date for planting. After harvesting the corn for freezing or canning, Green Giant sent us a check for payment.

One year, as usual, we made our arrangements with Green Giant and planted the corn. It came up in lovely green rows nearly half a mile long. We cultivated it and provided tender care. With plenty of rain from the Lord that summer, we expected a good harvest. We often walked through the field as the corn grew, just to enjoy the tall, lush green stalks and think about harvesttime.

Our contract with Green Giant included our stipulation that they would never send harvesters to the field on a Sabbath to pick the ripened corn. That year, the pickers came on a Friday. We explained to the field superintendent that they must quit picking by 6:30 p.m. regardless of whether or not they had finished. He brought in extra equipment and said he would do his best.

Sweet corn used for canning must be picked during a very narrow window of time. When the moisture content of the kernels reaches precisely the right level, it must be picked. A difference of even two days can determine whether the crop is usable or lost.

By our 6:30 evening deadline, only about half our crop had been picked. We would lose the rest, because the harvesters wouldn't be back in our area for a while. I watched at the gate as the trucks and the last large tractor-mounted picker left our farm. The picker driver throttled down his engine as he left and said, "Gilbert, you're crazy. We have working lights and can work all night to be finished by morning."

I said, "No thank you."

My wife and I experienced that feeling of inner peace and confidence when we do what is right, no matter how difficult. That Sabbath was special.

Two weeks later, the field man from Green Giant called and said he was in the area of our farm. He saw our remaining corn, and it still looked so green that he had again checked the moisture content. It hadn't changed from the picking date two weeks earlier. Would I agree to his bringing in the equipment and finishing the field? He said he never before had anything like this happen, and he could not understand how the corn had maintained its exact moisture content for such a long time. I quickly thanked him and gave the go-ahead to finish the harvest.

We knew the reason the corn had maintained its perfect harvesting condition. God had answered our prayer. He had rewarded our faithfulness to keep the Sabbath. And He had used that faithfulness as a witness to the

Green Giant Canning Company of His power and His grace.

Irene and I went back to college with our tuition money in hand and joy in our hearts. God is so good.

If you turn back your foot from the sabbath, from doing your pleasure on my holy day . . . then you shall take delight in the Lord, and I will make you ride upon the heights of the earth; I will feed you with the heritage of Jacob your father, for the mouth of the Lord has spoken. Isaiah 58:13, 14, RSV

Don F. Gilbert retired in 1995 as treasurer of the General Conference of Seventh-day Adventists in Silver Spring, Maryland. He graduated from Union College in 1955.

INDEX OF INDIVIDUALS

ABOUT THE EDITOR

Ronald Knott is a writer, editor, and public relations/fund raising consultant. After graduating from Atlantic Union College in South Lancaster, Massachusetts, in 1981, he worked for nine years in public relations at Andrews University in Berrien Springs, Michigan. From 1990 to 1994 Knott worked at the General Conference of Seventh-day Adventists in Silver Spring, Maryland. He is the author of *The Makings of a Philanthropic Fundraiser: The Instructive Example of Milton Murray* (Jossey-Bass, 1992), and the executive producer of *The Midnight Cry: William Miller and the End of the World*, a feature-length film documentary commissioned by the General Conference. He lives in Silver Spring, Maryland, with his wife, Esther—a pastor—and their daughter, Olivia.